British History i
General Editor:

continued overleaf

210

Please note that a sister series, Social History in Perspective, is available covering the key topics in social and cultural history.

British History in Perspective
Series Standing Order: ISBN 0–333–71356–7 hardcover/ISBN 0–333–69331–0 paperback

You can receive future titles in this series as they are published by placing a standing order. Please contact your bookseller or, in case of difficulty, write to the address below with your name and address, the title of the series and the ISBN quoted above.

Customer Services Department, Macmillan Distribution Ltd
Houndmills, Basingstoke, Hampshire RG21 6XS, England

POLITICS IN THE AGE OF FOX, PITT AND LIVERPOOL

REVISED EDITION

JOHN W. DERRY

First published 2001 by
PALGRAVE
Houndmills, Basingstoke, Hampshire RG21 6XS and
175 Fifth Avenue, New York, N. Y. 10010
Companies and representatives throughout the world

PALGRAVE is the new global academic imprint of
St. Martin's Press LLC Scholarly and Reference Division and
Palgrave Publishers Ltd (formerly Macmillan Press Ltd).

ISBN 978-0-333-94636-7

This book is printed on paper suitable for recycling and made from fully managed and sustained forest sources. Logging, pulping and manufacturing processes are expected to conform to the environmental regulations of the country of origin.

A catalogue record for this book is available from the British Library.

Library of Congress Cataloging-in-Publication Data
Derry, John W. (John Wesley)
    Politics in the age of Fox, Pitt, and Liverpool / John W. Derry.— Rev. ed.
        p. cm. — (British history in perspective)
    Includes bibliographical references and index.
    ISBN 0–333–94636–7
    1. Great Britain—Politics and government—1760–1820. 2. Great Britain—Politics and government—1800–1837. 3. Fox, Charles James, 1749–1806. 4. Pitt, William, 1759–1806. 5. Liverpool, Robert Banks Jenkinson, Earl of, 1770–1828. I. Title. II. Series.
    DA505 .D47 2001
    941.07'3—dc21
                                                    00–065212

Printed and bound in Great Britain by
CPI Antony Rowe, Chippenham and Eastbourne

CONTENTS

PREFACE

In writing this brief survey I have sought to provide the reader with sufficient narrative to make sense of what happened, while seeking to concentrate on a number of themes. I am grateful to Jeremy Black for inviting me to contribute a volume to his series; to Vanessa Graham, for her patience in waiting for the typescript, and to the University of Newcastle upon Tyne, whose provision of a term's study-leave greatly facilitated the production of the book.

Department of History   JOHN W. DERRY
University of Newcastle upon Tyne

INTRODUCTION

For half a century British politics were dominated by two men, the Younger Pitt and Lord Liverpool, whose assumptions were derived from the conventional wisdom of the eighteenth century but whose political skills ensured, not only that the country's traditional institutions survived a period of war and domestic change, but that the nation underwent transformation without experiencing revolution or sustained social conflict. Pitt established a particular mode of political behaviour, Liverpool reactivated it. Both looked back to the Glorious Revolution and the Revolution Settlement, with all that they implied in terms of the balanced constitution, but this did not mean that the political system stood still, or that they failed to recognise the need for adjustment. The defence of familiar institutions led to innovations in practice. Although Catholic emancipation and the reform of parliament marked the end of an era the Old Order in England ended on a note of achievement. The system established by Pitt and refined by Liverpool showed considerable resilience and a capacity for absorbing new challenges which has often been underestimated.

Although the notion that the country's civil peace and prosperity were the result of a perfect balance between the king, lords and commons was widely held throughout the eighteenth century the political system had never been wholly static. In the reign of Anne the conflict between Whig and Tory had been intense and continuous. After the accession of the House of Hanover, Walpole had given the nation two decades of peace and progress, but in the 1750s the political situation changed dramatically, and for the first twenty years of George III's reign there was much debate, not only over the American issue, but over the meaning and functioning of the constitution. The prerogatives and influence of the crown, the sovereignty of parliament and the nature of representation were debated in ways which suggested that the country was on the verge of comprehensive political change, possibly even revolution. The end of the American War brought further controversy. For two years politics were dominated by bitter disputation, and the crisis was resolved only when Pitt won the general election of 1784, convincing his contemporaries that the judgement of George III had been vindicated and the conventions underlying political conduct confirmed. Pitt restored faith in the Revolution Settlement and the political system associated with it. This did not mean that nothing was changed, or that the system was never questioned; it did mean that reform was eventually accomplished through constitutional means and on the basis of assumptions which were developments from traditional thinking, not a rejection of it.

Much has been written of the potentially revolutionary aspects of the period, of the combined threat from French ideology and domestic radicalism, of the dislocation and suffering caused by technological innovation, of the crisis which might have erupted in violent revolution but which failed to do so. While for some this might be a matter for congratulation or regret, it is timely to try to explain the strengths of the traditional system which enabled it to survive and to facilitate peaceful transition. It is also timely to look at the political system of the late eighteenth and early nineteenth centuries, not from the standpoint of those looking for the roots of democracy or the origins of the two-party system or the beginnings of a pluralist society or any other twentieth-century concern, but rather from a more genuinely contemporary viewpoint, when the working of the system was seen as dependent on a harmony of interests within the political nation, on a pattern of representation which was preoccupied with interests and communities, not masses or numbers, and on the acceptance of the legitimacy of crown prerogative and the conviction that the role of government was best limited to defence, finance and diplomacy, with the conduct of foreign relations being in some respects the primary concern of government.

Pitt and Liverpool and the majority of their contemporaries within the political nation believed that liberty and property were interrelated, each being secured and perpetuated by the other. The often heated debate between supporters of various administrations and their opponents grew out of a shared body of assumptions, accepted as part of the given order of things by Whig and Tory alike. Yet the utility of the designations Whig and Tory is itself questionable. Although they have often been deemed an obvious element in the vocabulary of politics their meaning was subject to subtle and significant changes of emphasis. The nature of the party system was less clear-cut than has often been assumed, and although the practice of responsible opposition was broadly accepted by the 1820s its emergence was more protracted and convoluted than simplistic ideas of a two-party confrontation assume. The landed interest remained the most important single interest, whose prosperity was regarded as fundamental to the well-being of society. But both Pitt and Liverpool were aware of the need to respond to the aspirations of merchants and manufacturers, whose confidence was necessary for the success of government even though it was taken for granted that they would be junior partners, not the equals of the landed community. Pitt and Liverpool were conscious of the new economic thinking of their day, but they grafted elements of such thinking on to a series of basic assumptions about society and the economy which were essentially traditional. What is clear is that the period from the mid-1780s to the late 1820s saw a common body of beliefs and a widely accepted pattern of political behaviour dominant in the conduct of the nation's public affairs. After the end of Liverpool's ministry this consensus fractured, never to be re-established in its traditional form.

This study seeks to explain what this consensus was, how it operated and with what success, and why it survived for so long. I have sought to bring together a number of strands, which have been well-covered in recent historical writing, in a form which may prove manageable for the student. I have attempted to look at the political system of the late eighteenth and early nineteenth centuries through contemporary eyes, without abandoning the perspective permissible to the historian who, unlike those about whom he is writing, has the ambiguous pleasure of knowing what was to come.

1

THE PITTITE RESTORATION

The Political Background

Only in retrospect do the 1780s appear to be an era of stability and achievement, with the Younger Pitt restoring the finances of the country and the confidence of the political nation in the conventional mode of conducting politics. When Lord North resigned in March 1782 he was accepting the final verdict of failure in America, symbolised by Cornwallis's surrender at Yorktown. North's fall ended a ministry remarkable for its longevity. He resigned without facing a formal vote of no-confidence in the House of Commons. Learning that the backbench country gentlemen had decided at a private meeting to withdraw their support from his administration, he was able, at long last, to persuade George III that the time had come for him to give up the seals of office. The King's response was wholly in character. He reminded North that it was he, North, who was abandoning the King, not the King deserting his minister. North's frequent offers of resignation throughout his twelve-year tenure as first minister had been motivated by feelings more complex than a simple desire to leave office, but there is no doubt that North resigned with a sense of relief. He had struggled hard to maintain British sovereignty in North America. He had fought to uphold parliament's legislative supremacy, which had been at the heart of the long conflict with the American colonists. His departure plunged the nation into a political crisis which lasted for two years, while his restored appetite for place and power played a dramatic part in the intensification and resolution of the crisis. Although the conduct of politicians – often wayward and almost always ambitious – heightened the feeling of crisis, the roots of the problem lay in the practice of politics as it had evolved in the middle years of the eighteenth century. The manner in which politicians viewed the nature and working of the constitution contributed to the recurrent difficulties which made it far from easy to find a minister who could retain the confidence of the king and command the support of a majority in the House of Commons. These were the conditions necessary for the formation and survival of any ministry. But because of the distinctive stage reached by the development of parliamentary politics it was often as arduous as it was elusive for even the most skilful politician to succeed in combining the two types of support essential for his continuance in government.

The search for the origins of the two-party system, and the obsession with tracing the emergence of a pattern of representation which could be regarded as preliminary to or synonymous with democracy, have long distorted the understanding of eighteenth-century politics. Historians looking back from a post-1832 vantage-point saw the eighteenth century as an age of deplorable corruption or imperfect and lethargic development. The best that could be said for the Hanoverian period was that it laid the foundations for later improvements; the worst that it clung to outmoded attitudes and questionable practices for too long. Yet nothing is more unhistorical than viewing any generation merely as the forerunner to the next. In any event, there was more change during the eighteenth century than too great an emphasis on the stability of the age suggests. Compared with the seventeenth century the reigns of the first three Georges were remarkably stable so far as the practice of politics was concerned, but this did not mean that the familiar features of the political landscape were exempt from all change. Indeed, the meaning and application of some of the best-known characteristics of eighteenth-century politics changed in ways which were impalpable and yet full of significance for the conduct of politics.

Among such transformations was the habit of defining politics in terms of a conflict between Whig and Tory. In 1715, Whig and Tory retained a distinctive meaning. The Whigs were identified with the Glorious Revolution, the Protestant Succession, a limited measure of toleration for Dissent, a more liberal view of the Church of England, and a sympathy for financial and commercial interests. The Tories were the party of the landed interest and the High Church faction within the Anglican establishment, with all that that implied by way of hostility towards Dissenters. The Tories found their greatest support among the country gentry. Although they detested the Church of Rome they were uneasy about the Hanoverian Succession, and misgivings about their yearnings for a Stuart Restoration proved their undoing in 1714. After George I became king the Whigs exploited fears of Jacobitism to discredit the Tories. Historians still debate the extent to which Jacobitism was a serious threat under the first two Georges and whether or not the Tories were indistinguishable from Jacobites. It is much harder to be sure about Tory support for either the Old or the Young Pretender than many bold assertions imply, but there was no doubt about the skill which Walpole showed in exploiting hatred of Jacobitism in discrediting the Tories. The Tory party survived until the 1740s, but it became less and less likely to gain office. Its psychology became that of a permanent opposition, and the party which had once defended the prerogatives of the crown came to manifest many of the symptoms of that attitude of mind which was designated by the description 'Country'. Suspicion of the executive and a belief that the country was becoming more corrupt under the rule of the Whigs, sustained many a country gentleman in his cups. The term Tory came to be virtually indistinguishable from that of a county member, and those Tories who yearned for office found it impossible to enter the promised land. The majority of politicians with an eye for place were Whigs. Bolingbroke sought to restore the fortunes of the Tory party by decrying party and affirming the necessity of rallying to the national interest, typified as it was by the king who was the father of his people. Those whose chief preoccupation was the attainment of power remained Whig in conviction, even though they did not always accept the designation. In the 1750s what was left of the old party system created in the reigns of William III and Anne disintegrated. When the young and inexperienced George III succeeded his grandfather in 1760 the terms Whig and Tory were irrelevant to the practice of politics.

Unfortunately, the mythology surrounding the first ten years of George III's reign obscured the demise of the old party system and led to a long historiographical tradition which accused George III of destroying the party system by breaking up each of the Whig groups in turn, seeking to revive the Tory interest, and allegedly reasserting the power and influence of the crown. The young king was seen as wishing to put the clock back to 1688 or even to restore Stuart absolutism. While George III and his favourite, Bute, were cast as villains, apologists for the two-party system cast the Whigs as heroes, the defenders of everything that had been achieved in 1689 and 1714 against the reactionary schemes of a bigoted monarch. But it is impossible to see the Whigs as a unified or coherent party or to accept the claim that the Rockinghamites alone merited the description of Whig. Whiggism had become so widely accepted that it was the fundamental ideology of several groups of politicians, each of which was in vigorous competition with the others for place, or involved in bitter controversy over issues which had nothing to do with the controversies of the later Stuarts. The Elder Pitt, Newcastle, Bedford, Grenville, Grafton, and Shelburne were all Whigs, but they were often intensely jealous of each other. By 1760 Jacobitism was a dead cause. It no longer posed any threat to political stability and the cause of the exiled Stuarts came to be suffused with a romantic sentiment which was all the more satisfying because it was politically irrelevant. Politicians quarrelling over the Peace of Paris, the Wilkes affair, and the American controversy discovered that contemporary relevance counted for more than constitutional principle. There was nothing uniquely Whig about the Rockinghamites, and much historical misunderstanding is avoided once they are denied their traditional monopoly of the term.

Far from seeking to subvert the constitution, George III came to the throne determined to defend the achievements of the Glorious Revolution and to do his duty as a constitutional monarch. His immaturity and inexperience were more important in explaining his behaviour during the early years of his reign than any deep-laid plot against the Whigs. George III had inherited the Hanoverian heirs' distrust of the king's ministers. He had imbibed the most platitudinous ideas about the constitution, believing that it was the most perfect of all human formations. What was wrong was that the politicians were not observing the rules of the game. The young George III saw party as synonymous with faction, and faction, in turn, was linked with corruption. He regarded the Duke of Newcastle as the foremost practitioner of corruption, carrying on where Walpole had left off. The king was deeply distrustful of Pitt, 'the blackest of hearts'. After the victories of 1759 he thought that the time was ripe for Britain to make an advantageous peace. He loathed Pitt as the overbearing and arrogant advocate of war. To harbour such prejudices was not in the least unconstitutional. Nor was there anything unusual in the king admitting his tutor, Lord Bute, into the administration. It was accepted that a new monarch would bring forward men in whom he had a special confidence. But Bute was an unhappy choice. The majority of politicians looked down upon him as a Scot, a political outsider, the feeble favourite of an immature monarch. Bute was incapable of satisfying the king's expectations. He shared his master's hatred of corruption, but he lacked the perception, good judgement, and political contacts necessary for success. But the Pitt–Newcastle administration was wrecked by its own internal dissensions, not the conduct of the king.

Two considerations are of particular relevance here. First, although by 1760 membership of the cabinet was confined to those who held the more important offices of state, conventions about the functioning of cabinet were defective. The long struggle between the nominal and the efficient cabinet had ended in victory for the efficient cabinet. But this did not mean that conventions about the appointment and dismissal of ministers and collective responsibility over matters of policy were as clear as they were later to become. Ministers were not always appointed together; their first loyalty lay to the king, not to the first minister; and they did not, as yet, believe it necessary for all members of the cabinet to resign collectively should the chief minister lose the confidence of the king or the support of the House of Commons. On questions of policy a similar latitude governed ministerial conduct. Ministers were expected to agree on issues such as foreign policy, defence and finance, but on many other matters disagreement was a regular feature of cabinet life. Mid-eighteenth-century governments did not exist to carry programmes of legislation. The range of government activity was limited to an extent which seems astonishing to those who expect governments to meddle in everything. Since politics consisted in responding to events as and when they arose cabinets were prone to fracture in open disagreement. Unanimity was respected neither in theory nor practice.

Secondly, governments were without a fully effective means of controlling the House of Commons. The majority of MPs gave support to governments only in the most generalised sense. They reserved their right to withdraw their support on particular questions, without this implying any desire for a change of government. Just as eighteenth-century cabinets were in effect coalitions of various groups, the loyalty of each being highly conditional, especially where the chief minister was concerned, so within the House of Commons the support of MPs was less predictable than was later to become the norm. In the first forty years of George III's reign, ministries had majorities in the Commons only in a tenuous and vulnerable sense. Endless negotiations were an indispensable accompaniment of political survival. Cabinets were continually being reshuffled or broadened; ministers sought to widen their appeal so as to embrace new groups within the House of Commons; and fundamental to everything was the confidence of the king.

In George III's reign general elections were an appeal by the king and his ministers for a renewal of confidence on the part of the political nation. They were not the opportunity for the electorate to instruct the king on his choice of ministers. The order of priorities was directly inverse to that which is habitual today. Nowadays it is assumed that a general election enables the electorate to choose which of the parties is to form the next government. The queen will send for the leader of the party which has a majority in the House of Commons, assuming that one party has such a majority. But in the eighteenth century the king was expected to take the initiative in choosing the first minister, and the majority of MPs were expected to give their support, in varying degrees, to any minister who had the confidence of the king. The king exercised a role in selecting a government which the queen would be expected to perform today only in exceptional circumstances, such as that of a hung parliament after a general election. The crown's political role has now become so attenuated that experts and commentators, as well as politicians, differ as to exactly how she should behave in such a situation, but in the eighteenth century virtually no one denied to the king the decisive part in choosing ministers. To his dying day George III believed that the Revolution Settlement had left the crown with two inalienable prerogatives: the right to choose and dismiss his ministers, and the right to veto legislation. Whatever controversy surrounded the manner in which the king exercised the first of these prerogatives there was no doubt that he legitimately possessed it, and although George III never formally used the royal veto (the last monarch to do so was Queen Anne when she vetoed the Scots Militia Bill in 1708), the king's concurrence in legislation was universally accepted as a plain fact of political life.

Not only did the king enjoy a decisive role in the formation of ministries, he was also expected to be active in sustaining them. It was here that George III's conduct in the early years of his reign was open to criticism. It was not that the king plotted the ruin of each Whig group in turn. Far from deliberately contriving the fall of the Pitt–Newcastle ministry, George III simply neglected to use his legitimate influence to reconcile the tensions which were tearing the ministry apart. His sin, if any, was a sin of omission. Kings were expected to reassure ministers, to persuade them to swallow their pride and carry on in circumstances of difficulty or embarrassment. George III, conscious that Pitt's advocacy of a pre-emptive strike against the Spanish bullion fleet had deeply divided the cabinet, allowed the disagreements to force Pitt to resign. The controversy had brought to a climax the conflict between the war party and the peace party in the cabinet. Later, when the Duke of Newcastle resigned over quarrels concerning the Prussian subsidy, the

King was again happy to permit internal dissension to destroy a ministry which did not possess his confidence. His choice of Bute as first minister once Newcastle had gone was foolish, but it was not unconstitutional. It did, however, allow politicians to assert that the King's promotion of Bute was the cause of all the troubles of the 1760s. Much of what was said about Bute was as ludicrous as it was vile, but the damage had been done.

Although George III harboured no secret plot to destroy the constitution he came to the throne imbued with a great dream. He wanted to purify politics, banish corruption, raise the standards of integrity and conduct in public life, and reign as a patriotic king, whose solicitude was the good of his subjects. The only thing wrong with the King's vision was that it was wholly divorced from political realities. The King was the victim of conventional wisdom, which descanted on the perfections of the constitution as a self-regulating mechanism capable of correcting any faults. Such faults as existed were, therefore, the responsibility of wicked and irresponsible men, who had abused power, exploited office for private profit, and preferred the prosperity of a faction to the welfare of the nation. Similarly, it was common to talk of the perfect balance between king, lords and commons, as if each were wholly independent of the others. This manner of speech misled the great French theorist, Montesquieu, into imagining that one of the virtues of the English system was the separation of powers. In fact the system worked because king, lords and commons were not independent of each other. But because it was fashionable to make much of the manner in which king, lords and commons each acted as a check upon the others, the sophisticated interrelationship between the king and the two houses of parliament was frequently misunderstood.

The lubricant which oiled what was a complex and far from self-regulating mechanism was one which its practitioners recognised as patronage and its critics stigmatised as corruption. In an era before MPs were paid, the distinction between corruption and a due reward for services rendered was bound to be an ambiguous one. It was through the exercise of the influence of the crown – manifested through pensions, offices of profit, both great and small, peerages, knighthoods, and promotions in the church, army or navy for friends, relations and political dependants – that governments consolidated support in both houses of parliament. Exaggeration has distorted perceptions of how this system operated. Patronage alone could not ensure a ministry's survival. It was more effective in rewarding past services than in determining future conduct, unlike the modern party system which seeks to determine how MPs behave throughout the lifetime of a parliament. Once rewarded by a baronetcy or a knighthood for past services, an eighteenth-century member could feel much more free in his response to future events. And eighteenth-century governments were vulnerable to the impact of the unexpected and the unforeseen. They were often dragged into controversies for which they were ill-prepared and conflicts which they had not desired. Governments had to be capable of rising to the challenge of events, especially as this expressed itself in the cut-and-thrust of parliamentary debate, if they were to survive. Patronage could not ensure an overall majority in the Commons; it could only stabilise a base which had already been built up by the arts of negotiation and compromise. One of the most essential skills for any first minister was the art of management. Less dramatic than oratory, less prone to attract the admiration of posterity, it was just as indispensable in procuring the support of a majority in the House of Commons.

In order to understand politics in the reign of George III the illusory model of a two-party system, comparable to that which operated in the age of Gladstone and Disraeli, must be set aside. Although historians have hesitated to extend Sir Lewis Namier's analysis backwards to the reign of Anne or forwards to the latter part of George III's reign, it still holds good for the middle decades of the eighteenth century. The House of Commons is best seen as being divided into three broad categories: the court interest, which supported any ministry which had the confidence of the king; the independent country gentlemen, holding themselves aloof from office but priding themselves on their willingness to give any ministry which had the royal confidence the opportunity to prove itself in office; and the various groups of active politicians, who were eager for place and in contention for office. If a two-party system was absent, so was any coherent notion of a formed opposition. Opposition was still frowned upon as being tainted with sedition, not to say treason. Most politicians rejected the idea that it was constitutionally acceptable for a group or groups of politicians to act consistently in opposition with the avowed intention of discrediting the government and taking its place. The suggestion that any group should force itself upon the king under specified conditions was rejected. Storming the closet, as it was called, was widely condemned, although it was occasionally practised, as by the Rockinghamites in 1782 or the Fox–North coalition in 1783. The king's freedom of choice, and his legitimate freedom of manoeuvre, were held to be essential to the efficient working of the system. What Maitland said about William III applied to the monarch in the reign of George III; the king was still a working, governing king, a king with a policy. He had to work with ministers who were acceptable to the Commons, and he was expected to respond to the mood of the House, whether over the appointment of individuals or over major issues of policy, but he was also expected to play a positive and at times a decisive role in politics. The king had to be capable of carrying out his duties effectively for the system to work: George III's inexperience and lack of judgement were therefore of particular significance in the early years of his reign.

But the young king quickly learned to appreciate the realities of political life. This was a sad and painful experience for him. Given the hostility aroused by the Peace of Paris George III had to call in Henry Fox to carry the peace proposals in the Commons. He was aware that by doing so he was calling in a bad man to rule bad men. The dream of purifying politics was shattered, and the last illusion was dispelled when Bute's nerve broke during the controversy over the Cider Tax in 1763. Bute's resignation marked the end of George III's youthful idealism. By 1766 the King had outgrown his dependence upon his former tutor. Although the King continued to correspond with Bute after he had ceased to hold office, Bute's political influence was soon negligible. But by corresponding with his ex-favourite the King gave a measure of credence to the legend of the minister behind the curtain, which allowed politicians out of favour with the King to blame their misfortunes upon the secret and malign influence of Bute. In some respects Bute provided irresponsible and incompetent politicians with a convenient alibi for their own failures.

By 1770, George III was one of the shrewdest politicians in Britain. During the crisis of 1782 to 1784 he showed a resilience and a resourcefulness which many a politician might envy. Although he risked almost everything, and pushed his powers to their limits if not beyond them during his struggle against Fox's India Bill, George III almost invariably reflected the prejudices and the convictions of the majority of his subjects. As he grew older he distrusted anything smacking of innovation, becoming more and more conscious of the duty laid upon him by his coronation oath to uphold the establishment in church and state. It is one of the greatest ironies of history that a man so obsessed with defending the constitutional settlement created by the Glorious Revolution should for so long have been charged with seeking to return to the ways of Charles II and James II, and accused of wanting to extend the prerogatives of the crown. Not even Edmund Burke, one of the most influential controversialists of the time, pressed such a charge. Burke acknowledged that there was no danger from prerogative. The danger came from the exercise of the crown's secret influence, a danger which was all the more potent because it operated beyond the scope of public scrutiny. In fact modern research has exploded the claim that in the 1760s and 1770s George III corrupted the House of Commons by the extensive distribution of favours on an ever-growing scale. The general election of 1761 was a conventional general election, neither more nor less corrupt than usual. The number of placemen reached a peak of about 250 in 1761, declining by some 20 per cent over the next twenty years. Increasing corruption, like the alleged royal plot against the constitution, was a political fiction, not a fact of history.

The notion that the electoral system was notoriously corrupt has survived longer than any other of the dramatic allegations made about the reign of George III by enthusiasts eager to justify the claims of the Rockinghamites or Foxites to be the architects of political liberty. Judged by the standards of later epochs the failings of the system were obvious. The distribution of seats favoured the south of the country; many of the boroughs represented in parliament were in decline, or in the grip of small groups of patrons or privileged bodies of electors. The landed interest was predominant politically as well as socially. Although the county franchise was uniform, the forty-shilling free-holder having been enfranchised in the reign of Henry VI, a qualifica-tion which was relatively generous by the mid-eighteenth century, the franchise in the boroughs varied with the terms of each charter of incorporation from the crown. In some boroughs the electorate was confined to the freemen or to members of the corporation, or to the owners or occupiers of designated properties, or to those who paid local rates, or who were not in receipt of alms, but there were a few boroughs where the franchise was actually more democratic than the borough franchise between 1832 and 1867. In Preston, for example, every adult male who spent the night before the poll opened in the town, was entitled to vote. With every year that passed the anomalies of such a system became all the more glaring.

Nevertheless, the majority of those who cared deeply about the representative system, whether they defended it or criticised it, accepted it and believed in it. Most of those who advocated a reform of parliament preferred to speak of renovation rather than of innovation. They believed that the system was sound in its essentials. By pruning away corruptions the pristine purity of the system would be restored. Reform meant the redistribution of seats, rather than the extension of the franchise. Only a small minority of radicals contemplated household suffrage, fewer still universal male suffrage. Representation was conceived in terms of interests and communities, not numbers or individuals. The franchise was a privilege, not a right. Because this was so, voting was open. It was thought appropriate that the unfranchised members of the community should know how those privileged to have the vote exercised the trust vested in them. In theory they were meant to consider the interests of the local community, not purely private concerns or loyalties. Open voting had the advantage for political activists that it permitted candidates and agents to know whether promises of support had actually materialised. But in the majority of constituencies general elections came and went without the formality of a contested poll. In election after election the majority of seats were uncontested, agreed returns obviating the necessity for an election. Since it was normal for constituencies to return two members, agreed returns were easier to arrange than when single-member constituencies became usual. Competing factions or rival families could share the representation and save themselves the cost and commotion of a contest.

Since deference was as much a feature of the political scene as it was of society in general, there were few objections to such practices, but candidates and patrons found that corporations and electors were capable of pressing hard bargains. Influence was integrated within a pattern of conventions which differentiated between what was legitimate and what was illegitimate. It was thought entirely proper for a landlord to have an interest in how his tenants voted; they shared a common concern for the welfare of the landed community and this transcended the passing excitements of political rivalry. What was universally condemned, though frequently practised, was the attempt to win votes by crude bribery, especially if the candidate doing so had no tie of family or residence or occupation linking him with the constituency. Electors were just as eager to be bribed as candidates were to bribe. It was one way of capitalising on a form of property, and the franchise was regarded as a form of property, not as a natural right. Improvements for the town were often as keenly negotiated for as purely personal advantages: property rights were seen as procuring community benefits. Similarly, those who had purchased properties in order to control a constituency resented anything which suggested that they might be deprived of their property. The contemporary social conscience was sensitive about the rights of property. To deprive a borough of its privilege of returning MPs to Westminster involved violating the borough charter and this was widely seen as an invasion of the rights of property. Once property became insecure, exposed to the arbitrary whims of the executive or the legislature, then political liberty itself would be endangered.

It was to overcome this type of objection that William Pitt the Younger offered a million pounds in compensation to those who would be disfranchised by the reform proposals which he laid before the House of Commons in 1785. He failed to carry the House with him, but the fact that he offered compensation showed not only the seriousness of his intentions regarding parliamentary reform but the nature of one of the most formidable obstacles in the path of reform. Similarly, when the Act of Union with Ireland was passed, substantial sums of money were paid out in compensation to those Irish patrons who were to lose their privilege of returning MPs. It is significant that many of those who were bitterly opposed to the Act of Union, and who remained so to the end, were eager to receive due compensation. All this demonstrates how futile it is to judge the late eighteenth century by twentieth-century standards. The British political system in the reign of George III was not democratic. The majority of those who were active in politics hated democracy as levelling and corrupting in its effects and as almost certain to militate against stable government. Of course a cynic might say that those who were doing well enough out of the system cheerfully sought to keep it as it was. But with all its faults it meant that government was responsible to the governed, and what was valued most of all was the belief that property was safe from the wanton inroads of an overbearing executive. Fundamental to the system, and one reason for its credibility, was the conviction that the individual needed to be protected from arbitrary government, particularly when such arbitrariness expressed itself in rising taxes. Radicals were as convinced as the most traditional of country gentlemen that low taxes were indicative of national prosperity and that high taxes were a sign of oppression, even of absolutism.

The Wilkes Affair

During the years 1760 to 1780 several issues ensured that conflict and change became a feature of political debate, even when stability and quiet were sought above everything else. The Peace of Paris was a good peace for Britain, but it was denounced by the Elder Pitt, John Wilkes and a wide range of commentators as a betrayal of Frederick of Prussia and an opportunity missed of reducing France to the rank of a second-rate power. The advocates of peace were unpopular. Wilkes created turmoil by the savagery with which he denounced the Peace and the ministers responsible for it. The criticisms voiced by Pitt and Wilkes were wildly partisan and grossly exaggerated, and the government deeply resented their ferocity. When Wilkes published a denunciation of the King's speech and the ministers of the crown in No. 45 of his newspaper, *North Briton*, he provoked a series of legal battles which eventually outlawed general warrants, thus securing a greater measure of freedom for the press. But Wilkes was compelled to flee to France because of the uproar surrounding the exploitation by his enemies of his obscene parody of Pope's *Essay on Man, An Essay on Woman*. On his return from France in 1768 Wilkes's election for the county of Middlesex outraged the government and a House of Commons which remembered his previous conduct with apprehension. Attempts to exclude Wilkes from the Commons only heightened his popular appeal. He claimed to be the defender of the liberties of freeborn Englishmen and of the right of freeholders to choose their own representatives in parliament. He became the champion of the people against a corrupt House of Commons and an overbearing executive. Radicals and reformers rallied to Wilkes, seeing in his struggle the opportunity to advance a variety of reformist causes.

Yet the alliance was never other than one of convenience. Wilkes was interested in reforming parliament, but only on traditional lines. Divisions within the Wilkite ranks meant that although Wilkes could embarrass the government, the Wilkite movement failed either to establish a permanent base for popular radicalism or to achieve any significant reform of parliament. But questions had been asked about the nature of representation and the health of the political system which left a legacy of reformist criticism which went beyond the issues originally associated with Wilkes. Wilkes himself became more conservative as the years went by. North allowed him to take his seat for Middlesex in 1774. Wilkes also carved out a career for himself in London politics, becoming first an alderman and then Lord Mayor. He was prominent in the suppression of the Gordon Riots in 1780 and ended his days as an enemy of the French Revolution. He had always been a traditionalist. The liberty he treasured was essentially Whig in inspiration. He saw himself as the defender of the constitution. Although a brilliant demagogue, he was never a democrat.

The American Dispute

Wilkes had also defended the rights of the American colonists, thus forging a bond between the defence of liberties at home and supporting the cause of the Americans, in opposing first Grenville's Stamp Act and then Townshend's duties. Yet one of the significant features of the American controversy was the emphasis placed by American radicals upon their inherited rights as subjects of King George. Several of the favourite themes of American radicalism were derived from the country tradition in British politics: that tradition which discerned corruption everywhere and which attacked the executive as the chief source of political infection. Most British politicians supported the legislative supremacy of the British parliament. The Elder Pitt was the only major politician to contemplate limiting the sovereignty of parliament. He disliked the Declaratory Act, which the Rockinghamites had passed as an accompaniment to the repeal of the Stamp Act, and which had reaffirmed parliament's legislative supremacy in all cases whatsoever. Pitt was willing to assert parliamentary supremacy in matters of trade, inter-colonial relations and defence, but to exclude from it internal taxation in the colonies. The majority of his colleagues disagreed with him. Even the so-called Friends of America believed that the sovereignty of the British parliament could neither be limited nor divided. Burke, who pleaded eloquently for reconciliation with the Americans, never doubted the legality of the British claim to tax the colonists. He argued that it was not always wise or expedient to exercise a right, however legitimate. Since the ties binding the colonies to Britain were ties of affection, magnanimity in politics was often the greatest wisdom. However strong the technicalities of the British case, there was more to be lost by offending the Americans and the British should seek to win back American confidence by refraining from actions which strained American trust in Britain.

Neither Burke nor any of the other Rockinghamite spokesmen had any solution to the long-term relationship of Britain and her American colonies. Grenville had tried to face the problem in 1763. All that Burke and his friends could urge was that by tact and discretion the British could restore the relationship to what it had been before the Stamp Act had stirred up American hostility. If nothing had been done to exacerbate American suspicions, this approach might have worked for a time, but the problems of colonial trade, the costs of defence, the treatment of the Indians, frontier disputes between the colonies, and the westward expansion of the colonies were all real and difficult. They had not been created by Grenville and they would not simply disappear. The British were caught in a predicament. They felt compelled to assert the sovereignty of parliament, the right of Britain to legislate for the interests of the empire as a whole, and their duty to support loyalist opinion in America. They did not want to precipitate a conflict but they could not yield to violence or condone sedition.

North tried to damp down the fires of unrest in the Thirteen Colonies by quietly dropping all of the Townshend duties except that on tea, but just when this policy seemed to be bearing fruit a crisis in the East India Company reopened the question of the tea-trade in America. What was meant to be a concession – a reduction in the tea duty in order to help the East India Company – was interpreted by American radicals as a subtle plot to erode American liberties and to deceive American opinion. The outcome was the Boston Tea Party. Since it proved impossible to punish those responsible for the outrage the government embarked on a policy of collective punishment. The Coercive Acts closed the port of Boston, suspended the Massachusetts constitution, and tightened up the administration of justice in the colony. They were intended to isolate the colony of Massachusetts from the other colonies. Instead they rallied colonial opinion, chiefly on the sensitive issue of charter rights. Yet fury in Britain over American extremism had been widespread. Even the Rockinghamites had been angry over the Boston Tea Party. Although they criticised the government's handling of events they had little to offer by way of a practicable alternative policy.

The American issue, however, was never as dominant in British minds as Victorian commentators imagined. But it had several significant effects on the pattern of British politics. First of all, it revived the radical cause. The problems of America were believed to prove all the accusations that the country was in the grip of a comprehensive system of corruption, which was jeopardising traditional liberties on both sides of the Atlantic. Secondly, it revived debate about the nature of representation. While the majority of MPs were content to exploit the familiar argument of virtual representation to justify British policy in America, more critical thinkers raised questions about the merits of the British system and the validity of the House of Commons' claim to represent the nation. Virtual representation – the belief that those without the vote could identify with those with similar interests to their own who enjoyed the privilege of representation – was a familiar argument by which the comprehensiveness of the traditional system was held to be demonstrated. Its applicability to the American situation was questioned, although it continued to be cited with reference to the British electoral system until the middle years of the nineteenth century. It was an attempt to rationalise a system which had evolved over centuries. Usually used as an argument against change, it was turned to a reformist purpose by the Whigs in 1832. As long as democratic assumptions were not regarded as a necessary precondition for theories of representation, virtual representation retained a measure of credibility for many writers and commentators. The American debate provoked some voices to be raised in criticism of the argument.

Even those who accepted virtual representation began to argue for some degree of reform to restore vitality to the political system. Moderates demanded a return to triennial parliaments and the elimination of the most corrupt boroughs, with a redistribution of seats to the larger counties and to the City of London. Radicals went further. Some called for household suffrage; others, such as Major John Cartwright, demanded manhood suffrage, annual parliaments, the payment of MPs, equal electoral districts, even the ballot – a programme which anticipated that of the Chartists by sixty years.

Thirdly, the American issue focused attention on the cost of government. The pressures of war gave conviction to claims that government was as expensive as it was corrupt, and that only a sustained reduction in public expenditure could restore the national finances. The cry for economical reform embraced the elimination of sinecures, household posts and placemen, and the reform of public finance. It appealed to many who found parliamentary reform too advanced and too questionable a programme.

Fourthly, the American War created the semblance of a united opposition. All who opposed the war in America could attack the government, demand conciliation with the Americans, and, once the war had widened to include hostilities against continental powers such as France and Spain, call for the abandonment of the attempt to force the Americans to return to their allegiance, in order to fight the war more effectively against Britain's European enemies.

In some respects the illusion of unity among the ranks of the opposition had greater long-term consequences for domestic politics than any of the other results of the American conflict. It appeared to restore something like a two-party system. North and his colleagues seemed to face an opposition which had an exclusive right to be called Whig and which appeared to offer comprehensive policies of reform and concession. The reality was less simple.

North and his Opponents

North's government was not a one-party government. It embraced a broad range of political opinion and its members came from several political groupings. Nor can it be described as Tory in any meaningful sense. North relied on the confidence of the King, but it is untrue to argue that he was riveted to office only by the ruthless will of George III. As long as the King gave unstinting support to the ministry North was able to appeal with considerable success to independent opinion in the Commons. But the government was not of one mind as to the conduct of the war. There was a division between those, such as Lord George Germain, who advocated a bold strategy to bring the war to a speedy end, and those, such as North and Dartmouth, who hankered for a less forceful and more conciliatory approach. Germain believed that only prompt and resolute action to support the American loyalists would prevent the war from becoming a conflict in which Britain would be fighting European enemies as well as rebellious colonists. Germain was unable to carry his policy into effect and, as a leading hawk, he became the scapegoat for failure. Those who favoured compromise and negotiation felt driven by American intransigence to make what they believed were tough responses to provocative radical gestures, but they hoped that a political solution could be found without recourse to all-out war. Just as Germain found no adequate means of applying his forward policy, so North and the other moderates in the government found it impossible to devise a policy of conciliation which could appeal to American opinion while convincing the British public that too much was not being offered to recalcitrant rebels. Nor was the ministry composed of men who believed that their political fortunes were indelibly linked with supporting North as the first minister of the crown. North himself was aware that his ministry was a traditional one, a coalition appealing to conventional middle-of-the-road opinion, which sought to retain the support of independent backbenchers, and which was under the usual pressures to preserve itself by making reshuffles to placate various groups and to broaden its range of support in the Commons. The ministry never sought to destroy the independence of the House of Commons by the distribution of patronage on an unprecedented scale. North's conduct in this respect, as in most others, was firmly within conventional limits. He was an efficient finance minister, whose handling of business anticipated some of the improvements later made by the Younger Pitt, but the ministry was always vulnerable because of the desertion of key supporters or the pressure exerted from time to time to prolong the ministry by the timely sacrifice of an unpopular minister.

What was remarkable was not that North's ministry fell in 1782, but that it lasted as long as it did. North deserved much credit for this. In many respects he had many of the qualities necessary for success in eighteenth-century politics. He got on well with the King and retained his confidence to the end of the administration, although his subsequent conduct offended George III. He was a good debater, able to defuse many a savage attack in the Commons by wit, shrewd argument, and a deceptively simple appeal to the convictions and prejudices of the country gentlemen. His competence in finance was self-evident. But there were weaknesses, and North himself was intelligent enough to recognise them. He was not by temperament fitted to be a war minister. He was conscious that his ministry was a government of departments; that is, that he was too willing to allow ministers to go their own way provided they met the rather lax conditions he laid down of general loyalty. Most of all, North was unlucky. He did not create the American problem; he inherited it. His attempts to pour oil on troubled waters succeeded for a time, but the underlying problems remained unsolved and probably they were insoluble. He was unfortunate that the East India Company experienced one of its recurrent crises at a time when the American question was unresolved. It is easier to see where North went wrong than to perceive any alternative policy which had a realistic chance of success. Until Yorktown most MPs supported North. He survived a major crisis in 1779–80 and won a general election which left him with a reasonable prospect of another term in office. When military defeat doomed the ministry and when the sacrifice of Lord George Germain failed to restore confidence in the administration, North resigned.

But it would be misleading to see his fall simply as a victory for the opposition. Naturally they claimed the credit and exploited the situation to their own advantage. But the fate of the Rockingham and Shelburne administrations revealed that all was not well with the various groups who liked to think of themselves as the defenders of the Whig tradition. Opposition to the American war had obscured significant disagreements. The opposition had never been a single entity. Rockingham and Burke liked to think of the Rockinghamite group as the essential opposition party, but there were other groups who prided themselves on their individuality. Chatham had gone his own way until his death. He rejected suggestions that the independence of the American colonies should be recognised but he advocated conciliation with the colonists in order to fight the French more effectively. Chatham feared that the policies of the British government would destroy the British empire in North America which had been his greatest achievement during the Seven Years War.

After his death some of those who had looked to Chatham saw Shelburne as their leader. Shelburne was an intelligent and perceptive politician, but he was a controversial and widely-distrusted figure. Intellectually he was more distinguished than most of his rivals. He patronised radical thinkers and he had links with French reformers. He had a sharper intellect and a tougher political brain than Rockingham. He was disliked because he appeared too subtle, too original, too devious, too difficult to deal with in cabinet or in negotiation. He combined a number of traditionalist attitudes with more radical ones. He befriended liberals such as Jeremy Bentham, yet stoutly supported the king's right to choose his ministers. He criticised North over America, but maintained that the Mutiny Act should be strictly enforced in the colonies. His ideas on the treatment of American Indians were too enlightened for colonial tastes. He was prepared, once the tide of battle had turned decisively against Britain, to recognise the independence of the colonies, but he hoped that the judicious conduct of the peace negotiations would enable Britain to retain useful associations with her former colonies. He believed that the Americans might see the benefits of a common foreign policy and a shared concern for matters of defence and security. He hoped that independence for the Americans would not prevent a common approach to the opening up of western territories or preclude advantageous terms for British commerce. In domestic affairs Shelburne was a staunch advocate of economical reform. But his motives differed from those of the Rockinghamites. They saw economical reform primarily as a means of reducing the influence of the crown, which they believed had been the cause of the misfortunes of the first twenty years of George III's reign. Shelburne was more concerned with improving administrative efficiency. He was indifferent over fictions about corruption but preoccupied with modernising the framework of government. His intelligence was not matched by ability to manage men, while his integrity and financial probity were questioned even by those with whom he sought to work politically.

Another prominent member of the opposition, who was to come into conflict with Shelburne on a number of issues, was Charles James Fox. The son of Henry Fox, one of the ablest and most notorious of eighteenth-century politicians, who was himself a symbol of the cynical manipulation of interests which has often been assumed to be one of the chief features of the era, Charles Fox had entered the Commons, while still under age, for the pocket borough of Midhurst in Sussex. Initially he sought a conventional political career, his eyes being firmly fixed on office. But his abilities were offset by his waywardness. He offended the king by his opposition to the Royal Marriages Act and compounded that offence by relentlessly pursuing the publishers and printers of parliamentary debates when North had decided to play down that particular controversy. The outcome was Fox's dismissal. He moved over to the opposition, not so much because he had experienced a profound political conversion as because he had little alternative but to associate with those who were currently excluded from office, once he himself was in the wilderness. The American controversy enabled Fox to make his mark as a brilliant critic of the policy of coercion in America. He also actively publicised the charge that North was the agent of royal corruption and that the influence of the crown was destroying the independence of the House of Commons and thereby creating a sinister imbalance in the constitution. Fox's adroitness, his extravagance in debate, his ability to mount a political onslaught with facility, wit and passion, his seemingly tireless capacity to heap insult, contempt and ridicule upon his opponents, made his presence in the ranks of the opposition one of the most turbulent and inspiring features of the long struggle against the American War. From an early stage Fox supported the Americans. Soon he argued that the independence of the colonists would have to be recognised and that it was in Britain's interests to do so. No military success in North America could settle the political questions which had passed beyond the capacity of any British government to handle. In any case military success was impossible: geography, logistics, the devotion of a free people to the cause of liberty, rendered any British victory in the field vain and futile. Far better, Fox asserted, to turn one's attention to France and Spain, and to devote energy and resources to fighting inveterate enemies, than seek to humiliate those who prided themselves as being the heirs to all the liberties of freeborn Englishmen.

North was one of the prime targets for Fox's eloquence. Fox affirmed that nothing could ever condone cooperation with the man who was the author of disaster in America and the agent of corruption and the erosion of political liberty at home. Fox was later to regret such extremism but he made his mark. Yet he never became a mere member of the Rockinghamite clan. He retained his own independence. His judgement often differed from that of Rockingham. He was more realistic, more shrewd in his assessment of political possibilities. While Rockingham stood on his dignity and made a complete change of ministry the precondition for taking office, Fox urged the wisdom of being more flexible in negotiation. He believed that it would be better to change the ministry, even if this meant working with former members of North's government, than to lose the opportunity for taking office by setting conditions which were too demanding or offensive to the king. Fox knew that he could influence events only by getting into office. Although his oratory flowered in opposition he longed for the opportunity to prove himself competent in the exercise of power. Perhaps he recognised that for his talents to develop he needed the discipline and stimulus of office. He was ambitious, but he was as realistic as his father had been in his assessment of human motives.

While in opposition he embraced several reformist causes. He was a staunch believer in religious liberty, detesting all laws which discriminated against anyone on grounds of religion. He therefore supported the repeal of the Test and Corporation Acts. Determined to curb the influence of the crown, he threw his considerable energies behind the call for economical reform. Even more dramatically, during the upsurge of reformist activity during 1779 and 1780, he had been active in the Westminster Committee, working with radicals for a measure of parliamentary reform. Yet Fox was never a radical or a democrat. He had little patience with pleas for manhood suffrage. His own preference was for household suffrage and triennial parliaments, and like most moderates – despite his rhetoric Fox was always cautious over parliamentary reform – he saw the key to reform as resting with prudent and timely redistribution. But he felt that it would be regrettable if the Rockinghamites allowed their own hesitancy over parliamentary reform to let slip the opportunity of building up links between the parliamentary opposition and reformers and radicals outside parliament. Fox recognised the tactical possibilities in the reform issue. He therefore subordinated principle to the demands of political manoeuvre, relying upon his oratory to blur the difference between himself and those whose enthusiasms he sought to exploit.

The fact that Fox appeared more radical than he was heightened the distaste which George III felt towards him. The King regarded Fox as the spoilt son of a selfish father. George III's conviction that Fox was an irresponsible opportunist without either integrity or scruple was intensified when the young Prince of Wales was swept into Fox's circle of friends. The Prince's dissipated lifestyle shocked his parents. George III found it convenient to blame Fox for his son's gambling, intemperance and womanising. The familiar Hanoverian pattern, with the heir to the throne acting in concert with his father's political enemies, was now repeated. The Prince became an opposition Whig. The King believed that Fox was as responsible for his son's political misconduct as for his debauchery. He also bitterly resented Fox's charges of corruption, his claims that secret influence was ruining the country. The King knew that such charges were untrue; he despised those who made them because he believed that they also knew them to be untrue, since every intelligent politician knew that all ministries depended upon influence to reward their followers and stabilise support within the House of Commons.

Fox was very much his own man. He thought Rockingham a limp and indecisive leader, acceptable only because the broad range of opposition politicians would serve under him if he ever became chief minister. But disagreements about political tactics, the nature and purpose of economical reform, the possibility and extent of parliamentary reform, and the relationship between parliamentary politicians and those who led popular reform movements, meant that there were several areas in which political cooperation was handicapped by genuine differences of opinion and a degree of mutual distrust.

In the closing years of the American War another figure made his appearance in the ranks of the opposition, William Pitt the Younger, the second son of the great Chatham. Groomed for politics from childhood, Pitt had failed to be elected at Cambridge in 1780 and had entered the Commons as MP for the pocket borough of Appleby. He bitterly criticised North's policy in America, hating those whose bungling of events looked like destroying his father's greatest achievement. But Pitt held aloof from the various opposition groups. He would work with them only on his own terms, and he was determined not to accept a merely subordinate situation. On several issues he was close to Shelburne, who had some claim to represent the Chathamite tradition among the opposition politicians. Like Shelburne, Pitt was keenly interested in administrative reform, improved governmental efficiency, the reduction of public expenditure, and a moderate reform of parliament. Like Shelburne, he was attracted to new modes of thought on commercial and fiscal questions. He admired Adam Smith and sympathised with the freer movement of goods between nations. Like Shelburne, Pitt was respectful of the king's prerogative, and the legitimate use of royal influence within the political structure. He believed that the king had the right to choose his ministers and to veto legislation. Like his father, Pitt was averse to party and to notions of formed opposition. He believed that the best government was a union of the widest range of available talent, working with the confidence of the king in the service of the national interest. As a powerful and eloquent speaker Pitt soon made an impression upon the House of Commons. He supported resolutions calling for a reform of parliament. In introducing a resolution of his own in 1782 he made it clear that he belonged to the traditionalists within the reform camp. He affirmed that the essentials of the constitution were sound, but that it was necessary for corruption to be pruned away so that the political nation could once more have full confidence in the country's representative institutions. Pitt straddled the conventional alignments of political life. In some ways a traditionalist, he was committed to reform; a critic of North, he respected the King; sharing several preoccupations with other opposition politicians, he nevertheless held back from fully identifying himself with them. He liked to describe himself as an independent Whig, and this was an accurate summary of his basic outlook. He did not, however, lead the Chathamite connection. In some respects that connection was dissolved. But Pitt's cousin, Lord Temple, was an active, bustling politician, fired by ambition, and the ties of cousinhood were to prove of major political import.

It cannot be claimed that the opposition to North was reformist, progressive or radical. Some members of the opposition were intensely conservative. Portland, for example, was always cautious in his attitude to reform. He was prepared to contemplate judicious economical reform, but parliamentary reform was always uncongenial to him. Similarly, Edmund Burke – an influential figure for as long as Rockingham lived – was never a radical. He was a powerful advocate of economical reform and enthusiastic about reforming East Indian administration and strengthening the control of the British government over the East India Company. Indeed, some of his friends thought that he was much too enthusiastic in dreaming up schemes of improved administration as a means of checking the conduct of the Governor-General in Bengal. More than any other publicist of the time Burke had commended the idea of party, but he had never fully worked out a formulated concept of a two-party system. His defence of party was primarily a justification of the Rockinghamites. Fox had learned the lesson, however, and was prepared to go further than any other major opposition figure in arguing that formed opposition was a valid element in the practice of politics. Even more ominously, Fox was brooding over the conventions of cabinet government. Although he had been more willing than Rockingham to contemplate working with at least some members of North's administration he was becoming more convinced of the utility of ideas of collective responsibility within the cabinet in strengthening the overall direction of government. Fox believed that one of the weaknesses of North's ministry had been that it was a government of departments. The time had come, he thought, to heighten the control of the first minister over the entire range of government. New conventions regarding the appointment of the first minister were called for. While most of his colleagues and rivals were willing to concede that the initiative in choosing the chief minister should still rest with the king, Fox was determined to give the cabinet a greater voice in selecting the head of ministry. For as long as Rockingham lived the issue was not an immediate one. It seemed obvious that should a change of government take place, Rockingham would head any new administration drawn from the ranks of North's opponents. But, without Rockingham, it would be by no means obvious who the first minister would be.

The Second Rockingham Ministry

George III had other ideas. Nothing was more offensive to him than the suggestion that he should lose his freedom to choose his ministers, and the first lord of the treasury more than any other. It would be bad enough to part with a minister in whom he had confidence, but nevertheless he believed that he would retain the right to choose a successor from the available candidates. When the King was forced to part with North in March 1782 he had no wish, in the first instance, to turn to Rockingham. George III believed that Shelburne was the best candidate for the premiership. He was intelligent and able, and from the King's point of view he had the additional advantage that he had never been associated with the more extreme posturings of the opposition. The King knew that Shelburne was sound on the conventions of the constitution, and that he had no wish to circumscribe the King's right to choose his ministers. The King approved of Shelburne's reluctance to recognise the independence of the American colonies at the outset of the peace negotiations. Shelburne knew that this concession would have to be made, but by holding back until it was apparent how negotiations were progressing he hoped to find it easier to get better peace terms for Britain. By offering generous terms to the Americans it might be possible to detach them from their French allies. If this proved impossible, at least their reliance upon the French might be weakened. It was not surprising that George III chose Shelburne to act as the mediator when soundings were made to find a minister to succeed North. Other opposition politicians were worried; it seemed that the King was making his preference plain for all to see. In fact, there was a general insistence among the opposition groups that Rockingham should head a new ministry. But Rockingham was determined to get the King's agreement to certain conditions before taking office.

First, Rockingham demanded a complete change of ministers. There was now no reason to submit to anything less than a complete transformation in government. Whatever arguments had been valid against a clean sweep in 1779 or 1780 carried no weight once North had resigned. Rockingham wanted a free hand in making his appointments. Secondly, he insisted that there should be no royal veto upon the recognition of the independence of the American colonies. Since the war had failed to reimpose British suzerainty in America there could be no shuffling on the issue of American independence. Thirdly, Rockingham asserted that the new ministry must be free to introduce measures of economical reform. Again, this was inevitable, given the consensus within the opposition that economical reform was absolutely necessary, whether as a means of limiting the influence of the crown or of improving the efficiency of public administration.

The King did not like the conditions. He felt, with some justification, that the closet was being stormed. But when Shelburne indicated that there was no viable alternative to Rockingham George III submitted to his fate. Rockingham became first lord of the treasury; Shelburne secretary for home affairs and the colonies; Fox foreign secretary. The secretaryships of state seemed the best places for the two most able and most controversial men in the government. Rockingham took the opportunity to abolish the old secretaryships for the northern and southern departments. There was much to be said for the change; the new allocation of responsibilities made better sense. But uncertainties about the relative duties of Fox and Shelburne led to much bitterness and eventually to the breakup of the ministry.

The administration took the initiative in Irish affairs. During the closing years of the American War the situation in Ireland had become critical. The Irish had much sympathy for the Americans; it was easy to draw parallels between the grievances of the Americans and the complaints of the Irish. The Anglo-Irish resented the subordination of the Dublin parliament to that at Westminster. Although their supremacy depended in the last resort upon Britain the Anglo-Irish hated to acknowledge the fact. The Irish parliament was monopolised by Protestants, Catholics being excluded, but many of those who were eager to affirm the rights of the Irish to legislative independence were reluctant to admit Catholics to public office. When Ireland was threatened by invasion, volunteer units had been formed. They provided a security against invasion and a means of putting pressure upon the British government. The Rockinghamites believed that the example of America meant making concessions in Ireland. They therefore gave the Dublin parliament legislative independence, flattering themselves that they had solved the thorny problem of the constitutional relationship between Britain and Ireland. The union of crowns was matched by the independence of the legislatures. But nothing had been settled. The Irish executive was still appointed by the British government through the lord lieutenant. Irish reformers wanted to reform the Irish parliament in order to reduce corruption and to make the Irish executive responsible to the Irish House of Commons. This raised a number of difficult issues. In the background was the growing awareness that while the Anglo-Irish claimed to speak for the Irish nation the majority of the nation was Catholic in religion and excluded from any share in the political system. In 1788 and 1789 events dramatically exposed the ambiguities and defects of what had fancifully been assumed to be a constitutional settlement. Although the Rockingham ministry ended amid acrimony its contribution to Anglo-Irish relations should not be ignored; it represented a dubious legacy with which a later generation of politicians had to grapple.

In any case, although the ministry had changed, the war was dragging on. By continuing to fight after Yorktown, and by gaining significant victories at the Battle of the Saints and the relief of Gibraltar the British were in a better position to extract more generous peace terms from their enemies. But it was one thing to talk in generalities about ending the war and recognising American independence, and another to show what these initiatives meant in practice. Soon it was evident that Shelburne and Fox were locked in bitter rivalry. Fox wanted to recognise American independence at the outset, believing that this would win American goodwill. Shelburne remained convinced that recognition should not be formally yielded until the overall shape of the peace settlement was clear. Shelburne was more magnanimous than Fox over the boundaries to be granted to the former colonies. But the responsibilities of the foreign secretary and the secretary for the home department and the colonies were ambiguous. Fox claimed that as foreign secretary he was responsible for dealing with the independent powers of Europe, through his representative Thomas Grenville. Shelburne argued that his colonial responsibilities made him accountable for negotiations with the Americans through his representative Richard Oswald. Fox believed that Shelburne was deliberately undermining the conduct of negotiations, and urged that Grenville be made solely responsible for handling the peace talks. The cabinet was wrestling with these problems when Rockingham died of influenza in July 1782.

The Fox–North Coalition

Fox was already out of patience with his colleagues. Rockingham's death weakened Fox's position still further; he felt that circumstances were moving irresistibly in Shelburne's favour. Fox talked of resignation; some of his friends, the Duke of Richmond especially, argued against such a step. It would not necessarily be the case that on every issue Fox would find himself in the minority within the cabinet and it would be foolish to jeopardise his career by a hasty resignation. Richmond urged working with Shelburne, whatever the difficulties. Only if such an attempt failed would it be wise to resort to the risky tactic of leaving the government. A petulant resignation would antagonise opinion. But Fox rejected Richmond's intelligent advice. Only one other member of the cabinet, Lord John Cavendish, the chancellor of the exchequer, resigned with Fox. Fox's resignation was an ill-considered decision. It was possibly the most grievous miscalculation of Fox's career and it was fraught with momentous consequences.

There was little likelihood of anyone other than Shelburne succeeding Rockingham. The King's preference was well-known, and whatever their misgivings, most members of the government were convinced that with Rockingham dead, Shelburne deserved the opportunity to prove himself in the highest office. Fox's resignation seemed the action of a man who had permitted personal pique to get the better of political judgement. The division within the ranks of those who thought of themselves as Whigs was manifest. With Shelburne appointed first minister it was hoped that royal confidence would rally support. But Shelburne knew that he would have to appeal to as broad a range of groups as possible if his ministry were to survive. Within the Commons Shelburne could count on about 140 MPs, Fox on 90, North on 120. The independents numbered about 100. The multi-group nature of politics was all too evident. Some form of coalition was necessary to preserve a viable administration. Shelburne also called up new talent, making Pitt chancellor of the exchequer. Earlier Pitt had refused any subordinate station under Rockingham. He had done so to maintain his independence and to raise the price of winning his approval. His gamble had paid off, but he brought talent to the administration, not voting strength. Like his father he ostentatiously refrained from building up a party.

Three courses were possible. Shelburne could make his peace with Fox, patching up the quarrel and restoring the apparent unity of the various Whig groups. Or he could turn to North. North's following was larger than that of Fox, and North's ministerial experience and debating skill would be of considerable value to any ministry. The third possibility seemed the least probable, and yet it was by no means wholly unreasonable: an alliance of Fox and North. Shelburne's own preference was for a reconciliation with Fox. Despite their wrangle over the peace negotiations they had much in common. Pitt was undoubtedly more inclined to turn to Fox than North. He had no wish to be party to the restoration of North to office. He blamed North for the loss of the American colonies, and because fidelity to his father's memory was high in his scale of values he felt deeply about the issue. Shelburne thought any chance of a reconciliation between Fox and North was unlikely. He therefore allowed Pitt to make an approach to Fox. Fox rejected the olive branch. He said that he would serve with Shelburne, but not under him. He reiterated his belief that the cabinet, not the king, ought to have the decisive say in picking a successor to a first minister removed by death or driven to resignation. His own candidate for the premiership was the Duke of Portland. Pitt replied that he had not come to betray Lord Shelburne. He knew that Fox was making a bid to take over the ministry. Portland's appointment as first lord of the treasury would mean that Fox would be the dominant figure in the administration. Like Shelburne, Pitt objected to Fox's claim that the king should submit to the cabinet's preference when selecting a first minister. But events had already moved too fast for Shelburne. George North and William Eden had initiated consultations for a coalition between Fox and North. Fox believed that this would offer him better prospects than a reconciliation with Shelburne.

At one time it was conventional to express outrage over the coalition between Fox and North. It seemed astonishing that the man held responsible for catastrophe in America should enter into a political alliance with the most bitter of his critics even before the American War was officially over. Fox replied to the charge of opportunism by affirming that his friendships not his enmities were eternal. Now that the American issue was virtually dead and buried he had no objection to working with North. He claimed that North was willing to agree to the right terms for political cooperation. Portland would head the ministry, Fox and North sharing the secretaryships between them. There was no doubt in Fox's mind that North would be a more congenial colleague than Shelburne could ever have been. North had admitted the need for a greater degree of collective responsibility in government, confessing that his own ministry had suffered because it had been a government of departments. There was agreement on economical reform. Parliamentary reform was left an open question. North was opposed to it, as were most of his supporters. The Rockinghamites and Foxites had always been divided upon it. Most important of all, from North's standpoint, was Fox's generosity in the allocation of posts in the proposed new ministry.

The American question was not the real difficulty. A much more threatening aspect was the vivid public awareness that Fox had frequently charged North with being an agent of royal corruption, and more recently he had accused Shelburne of plotting to bring discredited figures back into government. The latter tactic had been meant to pre-empt any bid by Shelburne for North's support, but to many observers it heightened their impression of Fox's opportunism and lack of scruple. He appeared to be doing precisely what he had accused Shelburne of trying to do. The conviction that the coalition was motivated by selfish opportunism was deepened when Fox and North defeated Shelburne over the draft peace terms. In one sense this was absolutely necessary from the opposition's point of view. Only if a government were defeated on a matter of major importance could it be claimed that it had lost the confidence of the House of Commons to such an extent as to be forced to resign. Fox was impatient for Shelburne's overthrow. But everyone knew that there were no realistic alternatives to the peace terms which had been provisionally agreed at Versailles, and men also recalled that at one stage Fox had denounced Shelburne for dragging his feet during the negotiations. Nevertheless, Shelburne was compelled to resign.

George III was bitter over what he regarded as the unscrupulous partisanship of Fox and North. It seemed the desperate gamble of men who had lost all sense of honour. He expected such behaviour from Fox; the coalition was only another example of his vicious lack of principle. But the King thought North's behaviour contemptible because it seemed out of character. He also remembered that he had paid North's debts; now his generosity was being repaid with treachery of the most lurid kind. The King tried hard to escape submitting to the inevitable. For six weeks he refused to summon Portland to the first lordship of the treasury. He begged several politicians, Pitt among them, to save him from the coalition. All refused. On a crude calculation it was clear that in the short term nothing could stop the Fox–North coalition. Finally George III succumbed with ill grace, harbouring thoughts of revenge, and refusing to give to his new ministers the usual signs of royal favour. They had stormed the closet; he therefore denied to them the normal resources of patronage. He saw no reason why he should give their supporters peerages or knighthoods or sinecure posts or promotions in the church or the armed services. When one of the first actions of the new ministry was to confirm the peace terms they had previously denounced, the impression of dishonest opportunism and a disregard for the conventions of political life was confirmed.

Yet the fate of the coalition was far from sealed. The King was antag-onistic, but he could do nothing unless a suitable opportunity presented itself. Coalition was a common feature of eighteenth-century political life. If the Foxites and Northites showed that they could govern, and if they avoided reopening old wounds or arousing suspicions about their conduct, they had every chance of surviving. They were strong in the House of Commons. But there were indications that they were less pop-ular outside the House. Fox's friend, Fitzpatrick, asserted that nothing but a period of really good government would reconcile opinion at large to the coalition. Caution and discretion, a willingness to court rather than to humiliate the king, and an avoidance of unnecessary controversy might have saved the day. Of course Shelburne and Pitt had defended the king's right to choose his ministers and had denounced actions which seemed to reduce George III to the level of the king of the Mahrattas, who had nothing of regality but the name. But whatever anxieties were felt about such matters there seemed to be no viable alternative to the coalition.

But the coalition proceeded to embark on conduct which broke all the guidelines for their survival. Fox was over-confident, complacent about his majority in the Commons, and contemptuous of the likelihood that George III would be able to do anything to prevent the ministers ruling as they wished. By raising the issue of the Prince of Wales's debts, and then attempting to tackle the vexed question of the East India Company and the administration of its affairs, they played into the hands of their enemies and antagonised those who had been content to wait to see how the ministry would prove itself by its handling of events.

The Prince of Wales was head over heels in debt. Now that his friends were in office he expected them to do something for him. Fox was happy to oblige. But the proposed settlement of the Prince's debts was fraught with difficulties. With the Prince reaching 21 years of age there were good reasons for providing him with a regular income. Fox begged the Prince to be reasonable, but when the ministers suggested £100 000 a year as the Prince's normal income the King was incensed. It is not certain to what extent George III was fully informed about the ministers' proposals, but he believed that £50 000 a year was a handsome enough income for his son. Eventually £60 000 were voted to pay off the Prince's debts and an annual income of £50 000 was provided through the civil list. The episode was a thoroughly unhappy one. It identified Fox and the ministers more closely with the Prince. This did them little credit with those who disapproved of the Prince's manner of life, and it damaged the government's standing with those who were looking for economy in public spending. The King was offended by the harmony of purpose which had united the Prince and Fox. The affair of the Prince's debts made George III all the more determined to rid himself of the ministry should a suitable opportunity present itself.

Within the ministry opinion had been divided. Fox was eager to reach a settlement, but he had the impossible task of trying to make the Prince of Wales appear both reasonable and deserving. Other ministers were anxious about the effect on public opinion of their apparent endorsement of the Prince's extravagance. Fox suspected that the King's hostility was inspired by politicians keen to discredit and defeat the coalition. He blamed Pitt for what looked like a stiffening of resolve on the part of the King. There is no evidence for this, but suspicions such as these revealed the stresses and strains within the ministry. North was always sensitive to the need to move cautiously. His followers were far less interested in pleasing the Prince than the Foxites were. Many of them, being by temperament men who liked to support a ministry which had the confidence of the king, were apprehensive about anything which would further offend George III. The incident heightened suspicions about the integrity of the ministry at a time when judicious moderation and a respect for the conventions of political life were called for, if the administration were to gain the goodwill of a wide spectrum of opinion.

If George III were to rid himself of the coalition several conditions had to be met. First, he needed an issue on which he could stand forward as the defender of the constitution. In other words, the coalition had to do something which appeared to violate the rules of public controversy. Secondly, the issue would have to be such as to enable the king to appeal for support not only to the public in general but to a significant interest group which could act as a focus and instigator of discontent. Thirdly, the King needed an alternative minister, someone who would be willing to take up office once the coalition were dismissed. It was not easy finding such an issue. Happily for George III the ministers proceeded to raise a question which met all the conditions necessary for the King to intervene with some chance of success.

Fox's India Bill

By introducing his India Bill, Fox initiated a sequence of events which proved to be the undoing of the ministry. Yet there were good reasons for attempting to reform East Indian administration. The East India Company had suffered from a series of crises. To many it seemed insufficiently under the scrutiny of the British executive. Among the coalitionists Burke was profoundly committed to the case of reform. His vision of India transcended trading accounts and ledgers. He believed that an ancient civilisation was at the mercy of profiteers and predators. Anything which held out the prospect of more responsible administration seemed good to him. He also detested Warren Hastings, the governor of Bengal, the man most closely associated with the policies of the East India Company. Fox was drawn to reform as the means by which British rule in India could become more enlightened and humane. But there were other, less noble, considerations which drew the ministry ineluctably towards intervention in Indian affairs. The King's refusal to make available to them normal crown patronage made any source of new patronage doubly attractive. There was no doubt that here the East India Company held out lavish possibilities, whatever its difficulties and whatever problems it faced in trade or administration.

North knew from personal experience that British governments had been compelled from time to time to intervene in order to save the East India Company from disaster. He remembered that his own India Bill had triggered off consequences in America which had been as unfortunate as they had been unexpected: a reminder that the results of political decisions were often quite different from those which had been anticipated. A desire to improve the situation of Indians under British rule, and a feeling that this worthy purpose could nevertheless be combined with political advantages, made the Indian issue irresistible to most members of the administration. Burke played the most influential part in drawing up the Bill. Its main feature was the establishment of a Board of Seven Commissioners, which would hold office for four years and which would scrutinise the conduct of the East India Company. By insisting that the Board be appointed for four years Fox and Burke hoped to make it independent of the shifts and eddies of parliamentary opinion. In one sense this was laudable: continuity would give a new sense of purpose to British policy. But the proposal was severely criticised. It was seen as giving Fox and his friends four years of undisturbed access to East Indian patronage, come what may. Nor had the East India Company been adequately consulted. The Company resented the Bill as a partisan interference in their affairs. In a massive publicity campaign the Company denounced the Bill as a sinister threat to charter rights. Their slogan, 'Our Charter and privileges are invaded, look to your own!', was a powerful rallying cry. Fox and Burke spoke eloquently on behalf of the Bill, and it passed the Commons comfortably enough, but North warned his colleagues of the dangers implicit in the situation. With his shrewd eye for political sensibilities North recognised the riskiness of the undertaking. A further problem was that it could be argued that the Bill's chances of having the beneficial effects on the life of millions of Indians which Burke and Fox had claimed for it were slender. It was easy, therefore, for the Bill's opponents to concentrate on the partisanship of the coalition, and although the ministry's supporters in the Commons rallied to the Bill it had still to face the hurdle of the House of Lords. Fox brushed aside hints that the Bill might get into difficulties in the Lords. North remained anxious about the outcome. George III had been biding his time. Now he had the opportunity to strike.

The King's patronage secretaries had been sounding out the possibilities of a general election, should this take place after the dismissal of the coalition. The signs were promising. In the closed constituencies there were many indications that Fox and his friends would do badly at a general election, especially if they were out of office. The controversy over the India Bill had damaged the coalition more outside parliament than inside it. Many reformers believed that the Bill had confirmed suspicions over the coalition's integrity on matters of patronage, suspicions which the dispute over the Prince of Wales's debts had already inflamed. The King needed an alternative minister. As an experienced politician he knew that there was no purpose in dismissing the coalition unless he had a viable successor. During the six weeks in which George III had tried to avoid appointing Portland as first minister Pitt had declined to serve. Now he accepted the King's invitation, but he stipulated that as a preliminary to the dismissal of the coalition there should be a clear demonstration of the King's lack of confidence in Fox and North. Pitt was wily enough to remain dissociated in the public mind from such a gesture. His cousin, Earl Temple, was given a letter by the King, which he was authorised to show to any doubters in the House of Lords. This letter indicated that anyone voting for the India Bill would be regarded as the King's enemy. Temple used his trump card to good effect. His intervention probably intensified a swing of opinion against the Bill which was already underway in the Lords. On 15 December the coalition was in a minority of eight in the Lords; on 17 December the margin against the Bill had risen to 19. This was enough for the King. In the early hours of 18 December 1783 he unceremoniously dismissed his ministers, treating them with a summary lack of courtesy which gave full vent to his detestation of them. Even more dramatically he called upon the 24-year-old William Pitt to be his first minister. The scene was set for a major political crisis.

Fox and his friends were understandably angry at the King's success. They talked of unconstitutional action by the King, likening George III to Charles I. They saw themselves as the victims of a foul plot. Yet they had done much to bring disaster upon themselves. During the controversy over the India Bill, William Eden, one of the architects of the coalition, had been indiscreet enough to talk of the advantages to the ministry of getting their hands upon East Indian patronage and of the way in which this would enable them to tighten their hold on power for at least seven years. Many saw the coalition as an unscrupulous gang of politicians who had stormed the closet, deprived the King of his legitimate right to choose his ministers, and then sought to exploit the East India question as a means of perpetuating their tenure of office. There was much exaggerated and lurid rhetoric on both sides of the controversy, but the anxieties provoked by the coalition's handling of the India Bill were genuine enough.

Defenders of the King argued that the defeat of the India Bill in the Lords enabled George III to save the constitution from men who had already disregarded the rules of the game. Even so, supporters of the King and of Pitt were less than frank about the reasons for and the nature of the King's intervention. They evaded questions about Temple's conduct by emphasising the legitimacy of the King's right to dismiss a government which had lost the confidence of the political nation on a major issue and the rightness of the King's appointment of a new administration. Pitt was content to let Temple carry the chief blame for the discomfiture of the opposition. He refused to be drawn as to the precise character of what had happened in the Lords. Fox asserted that if the King had wanted to reject the India Bill it would have been more fitting for him to have used his veto. But he ruined the effectiveness of this argument by saying that the royal veto ought to be exercised only on the advice of responsible ministers, which would have deprived the King of any chance of exercising it. In fact, George III had contemplated using his veto, only to put the idea aside as inappropriate. The veto had not been used since the reign of Anne; its use was bound to be fraught with controversy. More important was the uncertainty as to whether vetoing one piece of legislation would be enough to get rid of the ministry. Just as only a period of sound government could have reconciled the King and the political nation to the coalition's defeat of Shelburne, so the best justification for what George III had done would be a ministry which would match all that contemporaries required of it: a respect for political conventions, a capacity to handle financial and commercial questions, and an ability to restore Britain's standing in the world after the humiliation of the American War.

During the Christmas season Fox and his supporters were confident that Pitt would be defeated. They cheerfully anticipated that his ministry would collapse in ignominy and disgrace. Once again Fox was relying too blithely upon his majority in the Commons. He underestimated the political craft and personal resilience of Pitt. Fox thought that a series of defeats in the Commons would break Pitt's nerve, drive him to resignation, and compel the King, once again, to submit to the coalition. He also assumed that his majority in the House of Commons was immovable. But Fox was anxious over the possibility of a general election. He knew that general elections were invariably won by governments. It was ironic that a man who spoke so eloquently of the House of Commons as a check upon the influence of the crown, and who liked to represent himself as a man of the people, should distrust the idea of the electorate as a check upon the Commons. But Fox, whatever his flights of rhetoric, was essentially a parliamentarian, and as a politician his eye was focused on the prospects of power. He sensed that there were disturbing signs that Pitt and the King were winning the battle for public opinion. Meetings, petitions, and addresses supporting the King were more numerous, and better publicised, than those supporting the coalition. It was, therefore, essential for the opposition to defeat Pitt in the Commons and thus avert the danger of a general election. Fox denounced a dissolution as a dangerous abuse of the royal prerogative. The House of Commons had something like three years to run. It was convenient for the coalitionists to invoke the septennial convention, by which parliaments were not dissolved until near the end of their legal term.

Pitt did not want an immediate general election. The King had originally hoped for a prompt dissolution. Temple also thought a dissolution likely following the change of government. When this did not take place, and when the coalitionists talked of impeaching him because of his part in the defeat of the India Bill, Temple resigned as home secretary. So far as Robinson and Jenkinson, the King's secretaries, were concerned, all the preparations for a general election were nicely in hand. But Pitt was determined to face his critics in the Commons, and events showed that his judgement was sound. It needed considerable courage and immense nerve to defy the coalitionists in the Commons. Pitt calculated that if he could impress the House he would set in train a shift of opinion away from the opposition and towards himself. This would mean that when the general election took place the morale of the opposition would already be low. He knew that many of North's followers had been reconciled to the coalition with Fox only because it held out the prospect of a stable ministry. Now that this expectation had been dashed, many Northites were less than happy to continue the alliance with Fox, especially when this had earned the implacable disapprobation of the King.

Pitt was aware of the need to appeal to opinion outside the House of Commons. If he could show that his command of financial issues was assured, that he was willing to cultivate key interests rather than offend them, and that he was nevertheless interested in certain types of reform, he would rally both conservative and reformist support, both of which had been antagonised by the coalition. Finally, since his enemies asserted that he was no more than a front man, an agent for the King or even a stooge preparing for Shelburne's return, Pitt knew that by facing the Commons he would prove, in the most striking manner open to him, that he was his own man. He was careful not to offer Shelburne a post in his administration. Pitt was both first lord of the treasury and chancellor of the exchequer. After Temple's resignation Sydney became home secretary. Carmarthen was foreign secretary, Thurlow lord chancellor, Gower lord president of the council, Rutland lord privy seal, and Richmond master general of the ordnance. The burden of defending the ministry in the Commons fell upon Pitt himself. He welcomed the opportunity to demonstrate his ability to command events, to defy criticism and to outwit his opponents. As Pitt had guessed, he was able to win the confidence of the independents and of MPs who had not been closely involved in the struggle over the India Bill. Gradually opinion within the Commons moved his way. On the eve of the dissolution of parliament in March 1784 the opposition had a majority of only one vote.

Pitt also called Fox's bluff over the latter's threat to deny supplies to the crown. Had Fox carried his threat into effect one of two courses was inevitable: either Pitt would resign or the House would be dissolved. When Fox realised that the first possibility was out of the question his knowledge that a general election would be a disaster compelled him to refrain from using his parliamentary majority to bring certain catastrophe upon his own head. Pitt introduced an India Bill, which Fox and the opposition threw out. This was a clever move on Pitt's part. It established his own interest in reform, implied that reform of East India administration was possible in alliance with the East India Company rather than in conflict with it, and kept alive suspicions of the opposition's good faith on questions of reform.

When the election came in March 1784 the result was an emphatic victory for George III and Pitt. Probably about 90 supporters of the coalition failed to return to the Commons. Not all of these were defeated on the hustings. Some found that the tide was flowing against them and found it prudent to withdraw. Others realised that the price of re-election was to promise to transfer their support to Pitt. The election cannot be understood in terms of a straightforward swing of votes. The electoral system with its high proportion of uncontested returns, varieties of franchise, and sensitivity to regional loyalties and local interests was too complex for that. Nevertheless, all the evidence indicates a fusion of interest and opinion working for Pitt and against Fox. The real victor of the election was George III. The political nation condoned his dismissal of the coalition and confirmed his choice of Pitt as first minister. Pitt and his supporters did rather better in the open constituencies than had been expected and slightly less well in the closed ones. In some of the counties – Yorkshire, Berkshire, Norfolk – the hostility shown towards the coalition was intense. Lord John Cavendish never forgot the bitter loathing of the coalition which he encountered in Yorkshire. Even Fox found the fight at Westminster tough. Although he was returned he came second in the poll to Admiral Lord Hood, an avowed supporter of the King and Pitt. Victorian historians saw Pitt's victory as a popular triumph; then historians reacted against this view and saw the victory as a consequence of management and influence. It is now possible to see that opinion and influence were not mutually exclusive: Pitt benefited from both. George III congratulated his minister on the election result with pardonable pride and satisfaction. The King's judgement and ability to sense the mood of the nation had been vindicated.

Although Pitt could rely upon a majority in the House of Commons for most purposes, he was not in a position to carry whatever legislation he wished. The number of MPs pledged to Pitt was never more than about 50. He had to rely on the goodwill of the court interest and on those independents who were inclined to give a ministry which had the confidence of the King and the electorate the opportunity to prove itself capable of managing the affairs of the country. Fox had about 130 supporters in the new House of Commons. The main loser was North. His group declined from about 120 to about 70; within a few years it had shrunk still further. By 1788 men were talking of the remnants of North's party. Part of the explanation may be that many of North's supporters were shocked by the inability of the coalition to win the confidence of the King and thus establish itself as a credible government. Being by temperament inclined to support the executive, North's men found it convenient either to leave politics or to change sides.

Pitt in Office

Pitt soon showed that he had all the qualities necessary in a first minister. He respected the constitutional position of the King and frequently deferred to his judgement. George III knew that Pitt would not act in any way hostile to his interests. Pitt was an outstanding finance minister. In a series of judicious budgets he restored the economy, reduced and simplified customs and excise duties, and stimulated trade. He negotiated a commercial treaty with France which worked to Britain's advantage. All this restored the credibility of the political system. But there were limits to what Pitt could do. Few of his cabinet shared all of his enthusiasms. Virtually none of his colleagues felt that they owed their position solely or chiefly to Pitt. As time went on Pitt became closely associated with Dundas and Grenville in what was a triumvirate controlling the main direction of government policy, but this only became a marked feature of Pitt's style in the 1790s. On several issues – parliamentary reform, the slave trade, religious disabilities – Pitt had to accept that the majority of his cabinet and of his supporters in the Commons favoured a conservative stance. This explains why in 1785 his Bill to reform parliament was introduced as a private member's Bill, not as a piece of government legislation. Although the King kept his promise to remain silent during the discussion of Pitt's proposals, everyone knew that George III was opposed to parliamentary reform. Pitt had to appeal to the uncommitted and to the independents. This explains his offer of a million pounds in compensation to those who would be disfranchised under his plan to suppress 36 of the worst rotten boroughs and redistribute 72 seats to London and the more populous counties. Fox denounced the offer of compensation, but it represented a serious effort on Pitt's part to circumvent the familiar argument that parliamentary reform infringed property and charter rights, particularly of those who were to be the first victims of the purification of the system.

Pitt did not see himself as a party man. Like his father, he believed that the best governments were those which appealed to patriotic feelings and loyalty to the service of the crown. To the end of his life he described himself as an independent Whig, and rightly so. He did not trouble to build up a party. He preferred to patronise young men of talent, having a shrewd eye for promising men of potential executive ability. It was no accident that both Castlereagh and Canning owed so much to Pitt, a debt which both men never forgot. But Pitt had little time for the routine business of party organisation. He liked to present himself to the public as a minister who stood above the squabbles of faction. Similarly, he knew that if he were driven out of office, either because the King withdrew his confidence or if he were defeated in the Commons on a major issue, most of his cabinet would carry on under a successor acceptable to the monarch. Collective appointment and collective resignation lay in the future. Collective responsibility for policy was limited to finance, foreign policy and defence. This explains why Pitt had to endure Thurlow as lord chancellor for so long. Thurlow was the King's choice as lord chancellor. As the keeper of the royal conscience on all legal and constitutional matters the lord chancellor had to be someone who could command the unhesitating confidence of the King. During the Regency Crisis of 1788 Thurlow negotiated with the Foxite opposition; he hoped to keep his place even if Pitt went out and Fox came in. His behaviour was public knowledge. Yet Pitt could not dismiss him. Only in 1792, when Thurlow made it clear that he intended to oppose the financial policies of the government in the House of Lords, was Pitt able to force him to resign. Likewise, when the Duke of Leeds resigned in frustration after the Orchakov affair in 1791, this fell firmly within those conventions by which finance and foreign policy were the main tests of a government's coherence and credibility. Pitt was never in a position summarily to dismiss those members of his government with whom he had a temporary disagreement over a single matter of policy. He accepted without demur that certain political questions had to be left open. Ironically, several of these were of particular interest to posterity – parliamentary reform, the abolition of the slave trade, religious and civil disabilities.

This does not diminish Pitt's political dominance within his cabinet. Intellectually he towered over his colleagues. In the Commons he was a forceful and eloquent spokesman for his own ministry. But he recognised that there were constraints which he had to accept as the price of political power. He was always willing to work within them. Only towards the end of his career, after the controversy over Catholic emancipation had ended his first term as premier in 1801, did he come to feel that the pre-eminence of the prime minister needed a greater measure of formal recognition. He always rejected Fox's demand that the cabinet should have the decisive voice in the choice of a first minister. He disliked Fox's advocacy of party, formed opposition, and the reduction of the prerogatives and influence of the crown. In the battle against corruption he preferred to work by more subtle means than direct assault. When sinecures or redundant household posts became vacant he suppressed them or failed to fill them. Pitt believed that the conventions of the day were adequate to the demands being made of them, providing that politicians were willing honestly to work within them and to accept the legitimacy, indeed the necessity and utility, of the King's role in politics. By temperament Pitt was a traditionalist, but he demonstrated that traditional methods could produce acceptable results. He did not see himself as an innovator. Before everything else he was a servant of the crown. He was a committed parliamentarian, and only Fox could challenge him for the ear of the Commons, but he believed that the king and parliament were essentially in partnership. He advocated economical and parliamentary reform, but he regarded Rockinghamite tales of secret influence and royal plots against the constitution as dangerous and dismal nonsense. He admired Fox's oratorical skills, but not even the wand of the magician could make him accept Fox's claims that the ills of the day were entirely the consequences of the secret influence of the crown.

Pitt accepted several defeats with equanimity. Although willing to exploit any chance of future success, he never wasted time on futile repetition or futile gestures. This did not mean that he was a cynic or a man without convictions. He believed in parliamentary reform, but when it was defeated in 1785 he knew there was no chance of carrying it in the parliament which had been elected in 1784. He saw no constructive purpose, therefore, in reviving the question. He was a man who valued getting things done. He played neither to the gallery nor the populace. Yet he had as keen an insight into the temper of the times and the mood of the nation as any man. When defeated, whether over the reform of parliament or free trade with Ireland, he took stock of the situation, tried to see where his judgement had faltered, and sought to recover his political balance as quickly as possible. He recognised that he had to attune everything to the mind of the House of Commons, even though he was fully conscious of the limited perception of the typical back-bencher. When his attempt to introduce free trade with Ireland failed, partly because he had failed to consult crucial interest groups, he made up for this oversight by carefully consulting British manufacturers throughout the negotiations which led to the Eden Treaty with France. Few politicians were as adept as Pitt in turning a reverse into an advant-age, at learning from the twists and shifts of political infighting. But there were times when his ability to judge the mood of the Commons deserted him. One of the most notorious of these occasions was shortly after his great victory in the 1784 election. Fox's return for Westminster was disputed. Pitt pursued his rival through the protracted business of the Westminster scrutiny. Many MPs thought Pitt vindictive. Opinion reflected a growing sympathy for Fox, a feeling that Pitt was trying too hard to heap another humiliation upon his defeated rival. The only political justification for Pitt's actions was that he could not resist trying to expose the bogus self-righteousness of the Foxite Whigs in claiming to be free from any taint by making charges of electoral malpractice against Fox stick. In deference to majority opinion within the Commons, and to the great relief of many of his supporters, Pitt had to drop the scrutiny. What had seemed to be an opportunity to entrap an opponent had become an embarrassment. Pitt could do nothing unless he could carry the House of Commons with him along whatever road he wished to travel.

Throughout the 1780s Pitt governed in a competent but wholly traditional style. He was sympathetic to the ideas of Adam Smith and he appreciated the originality of thinkers such as Josiah Tucker or Richard Price. But he was no doctrinaire free-trader, however hard he tried to free trade from many of the obsolete restrictions inherited from the past. In constitutional matters Pitt was conservative. He took no new initiatives affecting the royal prerogative, cabinet government, the established church, or political party.

This does not mean that Pitt was the tool or dupe of George III. Although the King remained much more active in politics and more committed to the performance of his constitutional duties than suggestions of partial retirement imply – there has never been a more conscientious British sovereign than George III – for much of the time the King was so confident that Pitt would respect constitutional conventions that he gave his minister some latitude even in those areas of policy about which the King had misgivings. It appeared handsome of the King to remain silent during the debate on parliamentary reform in 1785. But the King's aversion to such a measure needed no publicity. George III liked the fact that he had a minister who could be relied upon to handle financial questions expertly, who was eager to restore Britain's standing in the world, and who had a due regard for accepted constitutional practice. But the King had no desire to be taken for granted, and Pitt was fully conscious of the need to respect the King's constitutional position and expressed opinions. The two men had considerable esteem for each other. Each knew the magnitude of the debt owed to the other. But the relationship was correct rather than cordial.

The Foxite Opposition

While on the government side Pitt's peacetime ministry was a period of return to familiar and trusted constitutional practice, it is worth asking whether the Foxite opposition was able to carry into effect any of those innovating ideas in constitutional theory or political practice which had contributed so much to Fox's discomfiture in 1784. Fox remained unrepentant. He saw the chief threat to English liberties as coming from the influence of the crown. The experience of the Fox–North coalition had demonstrated how easy it was for a ministry to get into difficulties if royal patronage was not made available to it, yet Fox still talked as if the distribution of royal favours was the cause of every political misfortune. The Foxites were acutely conscious of the extent to which their defeat had been caused by a shift in public attitudes. They assumed that some similar change in opinion would eventually benefit them, but they were inept in appealing to the public and often misjudged the popular mind.

Relations between Fox and North were good, but North was now a declining asset. The number of his followers in the Commons continued to dwindle and his health was deteriorating. By 1788 he was virtually blind. Yet he could still make as telling a debating speech as anyone, and in 1788 and 1789, despite his physical disability, he was called upon to try to extricate the opposition from the perils of the Regency crisis. The opposition came to appear more like a Foxite opposition than as the heir to the coalition. This strengthened the tendency of the Foxites to claim the exclusive right to the use of the designation Whig. In this area of controversy they enjoyed a decisive posthumous victory. Many historians have found it difficult to write of the Foxites without calling them Whigs. The Pittites, with just as valid a title to the Whig inheritance, are not usually called Whigs, even before the French Revolution brought about a dramatic realignment in British politics. To call Pitt and his followers Tories, however, makes the understanding of late eighteenth-century politics more difficult, rather than more comprehensible. The term Tory has all the wrong resonances, but because for too long it seemed natural to call the Foxites Whigs the temptation to call Pitt a Tory seemed to provide a neat and convenient way of giving clarity and consistency to the party differences of the period. Of course in all essentials Fox and his friends were Whigs, but to suggest that they alone merited such a description has led to much confusion. All the major political groupings were Whig. All politicians accepted the Glorious Revolution and the Settlement which followed it; all spoke with reverence of the system which combined the virtues of monarchy, aristocracy and democracy while avoiding the vices of all three; all prided themselves on their respect for parliament, the privileges of the House of Commons, and the benefits of the church established by law. Even when there were disagreements about the influence of the crown or the expediency of making concessions towards Catholics and Dissenters the assumptions of mainstream politicians were unhesitatingly and ostentatiously Whig.

In ideological terms Fox and his friends did little to advance Whig doctrine. All they did was to perpetuate myths about the influence of the crown which were increasingly irrelevant to the conduct of politics. Political controversy was carried on by Whigs who had fallen out about several current political issues, not about the essentials of the Whig faith. Even here the disagreements were more often the result of conflicting ambitions than divergent convictions. Fox continued to assert the need for innovations in constitutional theory and practice, but since he was out of office he could do nothing to reduce the influence of the crown, strengthen the cabinet, or make party more acceptable to the majority of the members of the House of Commons. Much of Fox's conduct harked back to an older tradition in politics: opposition for the sake of opposition. He felt impelled to attack Pitt and all his works. Often he did so from a position of weakness and with little understanding. On fiscal and commercial questions Pitt was supreme; Fox knew little about economics and cared less. Even in foreign affairs, which were always closest to Fox's heart, he often appeared erratic and wayward, swayed by the demands of political rivalry rather than moved by profound considerations of policy. Fox liked to assert that British interests were being sacrificed to those of Hanover. This was another old-fashioned emphasis, an echo of the reigns of the first two Georges.

Hostility to France was probably the most consistent element in Fox's outlook. During the debates on the Eden Treaty, Fox and Burke denounced the treaty as a dangerous concession to the French. Pitt was allowing Bourbon France to undermine British interests by a specious display of conciliation. Pitt replied by condemning the suggestion that Britain and France were predestined to eternal enmity: such an idea was a childish delusion. It was easy for Pitt to demonstrate that the treaty brought clear advantages to British manufacturing and commercial interests, and when the French sought to intervene in the Netherlands in 1787 Pitt soon showed that he was determined to check French influence in the Low Countries, even at the risk of war. Together with the King of Prussia the British government supported the Dutch Stadholder against the Dutch republicans, who had the backing of the French. During the Dutch crisis Fox criticised the government for not being more vigorous in challenging French policy in the Low Countries. Fox, who is often depicted as the advocate of peace at any price, was more bellicose than Pitt during the Dutch crisis. He claimed, with pardonable exaggeration, that his misgivings about the Eden Treaty had been proved to be well-founded. But when the Dutch crisis ended with the humiliation of the French, there was little Fox could do to turn such a conclusion to political advantage.

Opportunism was the dominant feature of Fox's behaviour in opposition; the opportunism of a brilliant but erratic man, who had the ominous feeling that the years were slipping away and that his chances of office were more remote than ever. Fox was ten years older than his rival; time was not on his side. The Foxites were driven along two paths: the first was to exploit their friendship with the Prince of Wales, the second was to improve their political organisation in the aftermath of what had happened in 1784 and in preparation for the general election due not later than 1791.

Turning to the Prince of Wales was another old-fashioned opposition technique. It recalled the old reversionary interest, which had led to each of the first two Hanoverians facing the hostility of his heir. Old-fashioned though it was there was something to be said in defence of such a gamble. George III was now middle-aged. It was inevitable that politicians should look to the future with the feeling that the future might not, after all, be too long delayed. Fox knew that there was no hope, after what had happened in 1783, of George III accepting him in office. But the reliance upon the Prince of Wales proved catastrophic. It had already created problems during the wrangle over the Prince's debts. The chief difficulty lay in the character of George Augustus, Prince of Wales. He was clever, sensitive, imaginative, with a streak of genuine aestheticism in his temperament. He was also vain, selfish, fickle, often indifferent to the truth and capable of sacrificing friends to his own convenience and comfort. He was unpopular, his flippant love of pleasure contrasting with the sobriety of his father, who was now highly regarded by the public who had taken him to their hearts as 'good King George'. A further irony was the fact that Fox, the enemy of the influence of the crown, was now relying upon the future George IV to undo the damage done to his career by George III.

Fox was unlucky in that his relations with the Prince took a turn for the worse after 1785, when the Prince went through a form of marriage with the only real love of his life, Mrs Maria Fitzherbert, a Catholic widow who insisted on being the Prince's wife. Fox had argued cogently and strenuously against such a marriage, but his pleas counted for less with the Prince than Mrs Fitzherbert's anxieties. She had no wish to be the Prince's mistress, but she was willing to risk the hostility of the public if her marriage was valid in the eyes of the church. It could not be valid for the purposes of the state, since it violated both the Act of Settlement and the Royal Marriages Act. The Prince could not marry a Catholic without jeopardising his chances of succeeding to the throne, and he could not legally marry without his father's consent. Fox warned the Prince, in language which was as compassionate as it was eloquent, against the sorry consequences of such a marriage, but after assuring Fox that there was no truth in the rumours that were circulating about a possible marriage to Maria Fitzherbert, the Prince married her ten days later without telling Fox what he had done. Nearly two years later, when the marriage was brought up in the House of Commons, Fox's forthright denials that such a match had taken place distressed Mrs Fitzherbert and offended the Prince. Sheridan was asked to pour oil on troubled waters and Fox discovered that he had been duped. He was fortunate in that Pitt did not think it right to exploit the Fitzherbert affair for partisan purposes. But the bond of confidence between Fox and the Prince had been weakened. Their relationship never recovered its former intimacy. At various times Fox and the Prince were not of one mind. Nevertheless, the reversionary interest remained fundamental to the conduct of the Foxite opposition in the 1780s. The advocates of innovation were compelled to rely on a tactic which was as questionable as it was obsolete. This was a measure of their frustration and evidence of the extent to which opposition was inherently futile and incapable of dictating the pace of public debate.

The Foxites were able to improve their political organisation. The Duke of Portland and William Adam were active in strengthening the links between the Whig Club in London and sympathetic patrons and interests in those constituencies where the Foxites were keen to maintain their support or improve their standing. Efforts to prepare for a general election were intensified by fears that the King might die in the autumn of 1788. A new parliament would have to be elected on the demise of one sovereign and the accession of his successor. The death of George III held out the best possibility of any improvement in the prospects of the Foxites. George IV would dismiss Pitt and install his friends in office. Fox hoped that at the subsequent general election he would be able to tighten his grip on power by reversing the verdict of 1784. If this were to happen George IV would have to exert himself as vigorously on Fox's behalf as his father had done on Pitt's account. Fox's objections to the influence of the crown were waived when it seemed likely that royal favour would bring essential political benefits in its train.

But George III did not die. He recovered from his illness – probably his first serious attack of porphyria – in February 1789, so Fox and his colleagues were not called upon to prove themselves at a general election. When a general election came in 1790 they did quite well. They prevented any further leakage to Pitt, but this did not get them any nearer to ousting him from power. They were fighting under two disadvantages, which their improved organisation could not dispel. First, they had cut a sorry figure during the Regency crisis, and secondly the impact of the French Revolution did nothing to shake public confidence in Pitt, although it had initially stimulated reform activities in Britain.

The Regency Crisis

The Regency Crisis represented a series of missed opportunities for the Foxites. The news that the King was ill had raised the spirits of the opposition. Their most determined opponent and their most powerful foe had been struck down. Even if the King did not die, the Foxites hoped that the Prince of Wales would dismiss Pitt and summon them to form a new administration once he was installed as Regent. But when George III's breakdown became public knowledge the Foxites were in an incoherent and scattered state. Fox himself was out of the country, holidaying in Italy with his mistress, Mrs Elizabeth Armistead. In his absence Sheridan, who was lodging with the Prince, seized the initiative. Most of the other opposition leaders were out of London when the crisis broke; this further hindered the formulation of an intelligent response to the crisis. Sheridan believed that it would be foolish to become bogged down in theoretical wrangles about regency. The quicker the Prince became Regent the better. Sheridan and the Prince entered into negotiations with Thurlow in order to allow him to retain the lord chancellorship should a change of ministry take place. This meant slighting Loughborough, their own candidate for the post, but they believed that the price was worth paying. Thurlow would strengthen their ranks in the Lords; detaching him from Pitt might be the first of several political conversions, and anything which broadened the ministry's base would heighten its credibility.

Portland, the nominal leader of the party and their choice for the premiership, gave no decisive lead. When Fox got back from Italy he was shocked to learn of what had happened in his absence, but he was compelled to defer to his colleagues' judgement. His health was poor. Wracked by dysentery, he had not the energy to challenge what had been decided while he was abroad. Eventually Thurlow failed to come over to the Foxites; this was chiefly because the medical evidence suggested that George III would, after all, recover his senses. The Foxites preferred to believe the gloomy prognostications of Dr Richard Warren, one of the King's physicians who was a political sympathiser. Nor did Fox take seriously the idea that there were legal and constitutional problems about the way in which a Regent was to be appointed and the terms on which he would fill the office. Pitt, on the other hand, took the King's medical condition and the constitutional questions posed by a regency with genuine seriousness. He became convinced that the King was not going to die. Once old Dr Addington, who had considerable experience in the treatment of the insane, stated that he had seen worse cases than that of George III recover, Pitt concluded that it was worth making a fight to stave off a Foxite triumph. He called in two doctors – the Reverend Francis Willis and his son – who claimed that they could cure the King. He asked the legal officers of the crown to prepare full surveys of how previous cases of royal illness or absence had been dealt with in the past. The outcome of these researches was Pitt's decision to impose limits on the powers of the Regent and to insist that it was parliament's responsibility to fill the vacancy in the exercise of the crown's authority by means of an act of parliament. This involved placing the great seal in commission in order to enable royal assent to be given to the proposed Regency Bill, but this legal fiction was thought an acceptable method of establishing parliament's capacity to act in the emergency. Although Pitt considered asking the Queen to be Regent in order to exclude the Prince of Wales from power, he finally decided that the appointment of the Prince, with limited powers, especially with respect to the dissolution of parliament and the distribution of patronage, would be the best means of defending the rights of the indisposed George III and affording himself the best chance of retaining office, or, if he were forced to resign, of minimising the damage his opponents could do during any regency.

Pitt was helped by the great wave of sympathy for the King which was provoked by his illness, and by the behaviour of the Prince of Wales, whose impatience to wield the powers of the crown revealed a deplorable lack of concern for his father's plight. Fox assumed too lightly that the appointment of the Prince of Wales was only a matter of time, and that Pitt's delaying tactics were as futile as they were contemptible. In the debate in the Commons on 10 December 1788 Fox committed a decisive blunder. Without consulting his colleagues, or informing them of what he intended to say, he asserted that the Prince of Wales had an inherent right to the regency. This affirmation played into Pitt's hands. As Fox was speaking Pitt slapped his thigh and told his neighbour on the front bench that he would unwhig Fox for life. Fox realised his mistake and tried to limit the damage by saying that parliament could say when the Prince should exercise the right to which he was entitled, but his dismissal of the relevance of any precedents antagonised the House and gave Pitt an opening which he exploited with promptitude and skill. Worst of all, it seemed to many MPs that Fox was eager to abandon Whig principles when party advantage made such a sacrifice convenient. Throughout the crisis Pitt won acclaim as the champion, not only of the rights of George III, but also of the privileges of parliament. Fox was exposed as an opportunist, asserting the prerogatives of the crown in language evocative of the royalism of the seventeenth century. The man of the people seemed to have been transformed into a reactionary. Not even the intervention of Lord North – now blind and virtually in political retirement – could salvage the Foxite cause.

The Foxite opposition was bitterly divided. Portland dithered; Fox floundered; Sheridan's pragmatism, although explicable, only tied the party more firmly to the cause of the Prince of Wales. Thurlow, with his keen nose for movements of political opinion, decided not to rat. Loughborough, bitterly resentful over the disloyalty of his friends, felt free to take whatever action might prove necessary for the advancement of his own career. His colleagues had ignored his feelings; now he could ignore theirs. Most significantly of all, both for the course of the regency debates and the future of the party, Edmund Burke decided that the issues raised by the regency were so fundamental that he intervened in parliament in order to reaffirm the Prince's inherent right just when his colleagues were doing their best to escape from the consequences of asserting such a doctrine. Ever since the death of Rockingham Burke had been a lonely figure. The *débâcle* of the India Bill had led many of the Foxites to cite Burke as the author of the catastrophe. The India Bill had largely been his work; he was therefore blamed for the misfortunes of the party. But now Burke was indifferent to the fate of a mere party. Even before the French Revolution broke out he saw himself as the sole custodian of the Whig tradition. Shallow opportunism had corrupted his colleagues' devotion to pure Whig principles, just as love of place had led Pitt to place personal advantage above fidelity to the principles of the constitution. Burke was already moving in those realms of abstraction to which most politicians were strangers. The obsessional element in his personality was strikingly evident. He shocked MPs by lecturing them at great length and in lurid detail about the varieties and treatment of mental illness; he bored them by making the defence of the Prince's right to regency the occasion of loquacious expositions of the sanctity of the hereditary principle. Burke maintained that the hereditary principle was fundamental to the constitution. To deny the Prince's inherent right was tantamount to establishing a precedent for unconstitutional conduct and specious opportunism.

When George III recovered, the Foxites were in a miserable condition. Far from bringing them closer to power, their reliance upon the Prince of Wales had led to defeat and humiliation. Pitt was all the more securely entrenched in power. Not only had he won the parliamentary struggle, he had also emerged as the clear victor in the popular controversy which had accompanied the regency debates. Reformers were convinced that Fox's errors of judgement and wilful yearning for office had made him an unreliable protagonist even for those causes, such as the reform of parliament and the repeal of the Test and Corporation Acts, to which he was consistently and honourably pledged. The younger Foxites, of whom Charles Grey was one of the most able and most ambitious, bitterly criticised Fox's poor leadership during the Regency affair. Even as warm an admirer of Fox as the Duchess of Devonshire had grave misgivings about him. Portland had been inept, despite his work in restoring party organisation. Burke retired into gloomy isolation, depressed by the failure of his colleagues to rise to the challenge of events. Loughborough, who, like Burke, sincerely believed in the doctrine of the Prince's inherent right, felt slighted and wronged. The party had lost the one virtue to which it might appeal, whatever its prospects: fidelity to the dubious but valuable notion that it alone was the guarantor of Whig ideas. The Prince was more unpopular than ever, and during the King's illness further questions had been asked about the Prince's rumoured marriage. When George III resumed his duties in the spring of 1789 he was fully aware that Pitt had done everything to protect his interests and to make it easy for him to take his normal place in public life once his health had been restored. This made the callous indifference of his eldest son and the feckless impatience of his son's friends all the more galling. On the eve of the French Revolution the Foxites were divided, depressed, an object of derision among those reformist circles which Fox liked to court, and the recipients of disgust on the part of those whose first loyalty lay to the King.

The Foxites had reaped the bitter harvest of their own misjudge-ments, but their frustrations reflected the extent to which Pitt had succeeded, not only in restoring the fiscal, commercial and diplomatic fortunes of the country, but in reinvigorating the traditional pattern of politics. No longer was it widely felt that the political system suffered from fundamental defects. With the King's confidence as the firm base for his political power Pitt had won the support of the House of Commons on a wide range of issues, especially those which were central to the survival of any government. This was much more significant than the reverses Pitt had been forced to accept. Even those who disliked Pitt's proposals for Irish free trade or parliamentary reform, or who were unhappy about the possible removal of traditional religious disabil-ities, could nevertheless see that his administration was true to the main-stream of conventional thinking and that it had amply proved its competence in finance, commerce and foreign relations. Commercial success bred new confidence. In 1787 the French had been defeated in the Low Countries without a war. In 1788 the Triple Alliance with Prussia and the Netherlands had ended a quarter of a century of diplomatic isolation. Pitt had achieved all this without infringing the rights of the King. Indeed, his respect for the King's rights had been one of the principal ingredients in explaining his success during the incapacity of George III.

Nor had Pitt trampled on the rights of ministers or sought in any novel or improper sense to utilise crown patronage to establish a personal party. His dominance in politics seemed an endorsement of traditional values. The manner in which he bore himself in triumph confirmed the belief of backbench MPs that the body politic was sound and that in Pitt the nation had a first minister who could be trusted to make the traditional system work. Doubts and anxieties which had been engendered by defeat in the war in America – most of all the feeling that the loss of the Thirteen Colonies had reflected a deep-seated malaise in the country's political institutions – had been laid to rest. Working within the contemporary administrative structure Pitt had demonstrated that cautious economical reform both saved money and improved the efficiency of public administration. Paradoxically, all this meant that by the end of the 1780s the fire and the fury had gone out of the British reform movement. The middle ground in politics shrank from any tampering with the system. After the Regency Crisis, Fox's novel ideas about collective responsibility, the method of choosing a first minister, and the practice of formed opposition and party politics were rejected as questionable gestures on the part of a politician whose chief motive was a thirst for power, but whose defective judgement disqualified him from receiving the trust necessary for the exercise of power. In a system which depended upon a generous measure of mutual confidence among those who sought to act together in politics the Foxites found themselves embittered and distrustful, their self-esteem shattered, despite the powerful charm which Fox still exercised personally. To anyone who thought seriously about the balance of the constitution, the rights of king, lords and commons, and the need for a first minister to retain the confidence of the king while possessing the respect of his colleagues and the support of the House of Commons, there was little doubt that it was Pitt, not Fox, who was the more dependable custodian of the Whig constitution. Soon events challenged the British people into renewing their defence of their traditional institutions, and once more it was Pitt, not Fox, who was widely regarded as the pilot to weather the storm.

2

THE CHALLENGE OF WAR

In the spring of 1789 the prevalent mood in Britain was one of celebration. The recovery of George III was greeted with widespread relief; the nation rejoiced at being delivered from crisis. Pitt had once again demonstrated his uncanny mastery of the craft of politics. Only Fox and his friends ruefully brooded over the collapse of their hopes. The news that the States-General were meeting in Versailles heightened the feeling of optimism. It seemed almost beyond belief that the Bourbon monarchy, for so long the symbol to most Britons of absolutism and intolerance, was on the brink of reforming itself.

The Impact of the French Revolution

Early reactions to the French Revolution were overwhelmingly favourable. Whatever problems the French might encounter in framing a constitution for themselves, it was thought that the outcome would be a constitutional monarchy on the English model. The French appeared to be imitating Britain, and this was universally regarded with approval. Pitt was by no means opposed to reform in France. He believed that reform would mean that the new French regime would be less likely to embark on aggressive or warlike policies. The cautious rapprochement with France which had been reflected in a limited way in the Eden Treaty would be confirmed and developed. The French would be too preoccupied with their domestic affairs to repeat the adventurism of the Dutch crisis. So far as the British government was concerned, sympathy for the cause of reform in France was tinged with condescension and complacency.

Fox and the opposition were enthusiastic about the revolution in France. 'How much the greatest event in the history of the world, and how much the best!' Fox exclaimed on hearing of the fall of the Bastille. The Foxites were especially delighted over the establishment of religious toleration in France and the abolition of religious tests for public office. Here the French were doing more than imitating the English; they were going farther and more quickly down the road to full civil equality. That, and the assumption that the French reformers would soon set up a viable system of representative and responsible government, allowed Fox to feel that, however gloomy the prospect in Britain was for his brand of Whiggism, the future in France was more promising.

Radicals and Dissenters rejoiced at the collapse of French absolutism, the limitation of the privileges of the Catholic Church in France, and the proclamation of civil and political equality without regard to religious affiliations. Men who had been disappointed by the failure of the campaign to repeal the Test and Corporation Acts and depressed by the slowingdown of any momentum in Britain towards even a modest measure of parliamentary reform looked to events in France as a timely example of necessary reform and a welcome stimulus to renewed efforts to achieve reform in England. Virtually no one expected that the French Revolution would plunge Europe into a generation of war and conflict.

Many of the consequences in Britain usually attributed to the French Revolution were more directly connected with the great war which began in 1792, in which Britain became involved in 1793. Pitt was determined to maintain a staunchly neutral stance for as long as possible. He had no desire to become entangled in French domestic politics; he was aware that their endless complexities were beyond his control. He and his colleagues agreed that the best policy for Britain was to remain aloof; it was for the French to sort out their own problems. George III initially contented himself with reflecting that the embarrassments facing Louis XVI were a just retribution for the encouragement which the King of France had given to the American rebels. Later George III was deeply moved by the sufferings of the French royal family and outraged by the executions of Louis XVI and Marie Antoinette. But in the spring and summer of 1789 there was no real sense of anxiety in Britain. Concern was expressed over outbursts of mob violence, but these seemed deplorable excesses, regrettable examples of the brutality of life under the *ancien régime*, rather than clues to the deeper meaning of the Revolution. Even when France was torn apart by civil strife Pitt thought that France was the object of pity, even to a rival. He struggled long and hard to avoid any confrontation with France and any involvement in European hostilities.

However dramatic the events of 1789 in France – the Tennis Court Oath, the transformation of the States-General into the National Assembly, the Declaration of the Rights of Man, the attack on clerical and aristocratic privileges, the fall of the Bastille, the March of the Women, unrest in the provinces – it was an event in London in the autumn of that year which had the most momentous consequences for the development of the controversy in Britain over the course of events in France. English reformers were conscious that 1789 was the centenary of the English Bill of Rights. They were eager to celebrate the Glorious Revolution of 1688 and to draw parallels between Britain and France in such a manner as to put new heart into reformist causes. In November 1789 the Reverend Dr Richard Price, a noted Dissenter and a well-known commentator on public affairs, preached a sermon which was widely publicised and lavishly praised in radical circles. Price took the opportunity to draw analogies between Britain, America and France. As an apologist for the American cause he spoke in glowing eloquence of the way in which enlightenment was spreading from one continent to another. Mankind was on the verge of a great era of reform and progress. The example of America had inspired the French; now the English could brace themselves to take up the cause of reform. Good though the Revolution of 1688 had been it was imperfect; the Revolution Settlement was incomplete. Religious disabilities disfigured the British system. Now the time had come to sweep away the last vestiges of religious discrimination. Price spoke as a keen advocate of economical reform, free trade, the reform of parliament and international peace. He went so far as to paraphrase the *Nunc Dimittis* when expressing his joy at the contemporary scene. What was happening in France was little less than a miracle. Price was not alone in harbouring such sentiments. But his analysis of the Revolution of 1688 and its significance was so radical in its implications that Burke was provoked to challenge it. Price's sermon convinced Burke that the true principles of the Whig creed were being betrayed in every quarter, and especially by those who claimed to cherish them – not only by Pitt and Fox but now by radicals and Dissenters. Price had claimed that the Revolution of 1688 had shown that the British people had the right to frame a government for themselves and to cashier their governors for misconduct. What the English had once done the French were now doing. It was both sensible and possible to scrap the remnants of past folly and to begin afresh. Price exaggerated the novelty of what had happened in 1688 and 1689, played down the conservatism of the Glorious Revolution, and sought to make it a suitable inspiration for radical innovations, whether in France or England.

The Intervention of Burke

Burke was not opposed to reform in France. He recognised the defects of the *ancien régime*. But much of what had been said and done in the summer and autumn of 1789 struck him as ill-advised and dangerous. Judicious reform was desirable; doctrinaire extremism, unrealistic utopianism, violent fanaticism were to be abhorred. Burke believed that the secret of the success of the English Revolution had been its caution. Instead of rejecting the past the men of 1688 had built upon it. James II had threatened the constitution and the liberties of the country by his rash and innovatory policies. It had, therefore, been necessary to get rid of him. But Burke singled out for praise the manner in which change had been carefully limited to what was absolutely unavoidable. To secure the Protestant religion established by law it had been necessary to depart from the strict line of hereditary descent in providing for the succession to the crown, but the change in the dynasty had been prudently circumscribed, and there had been no suggestion that the nation was being given a wholly new set of governmental institutions. The errors of the Commonwealth and the Protectorate had not been repeated. The Bill of Rights was intended to safeguard liberties inherited from the past, as well as to prevent any repetition of the abuse of royal powers in any manner reminiscent of James II. A Protestant succession was necessary for the security of a Protestant kingdom. The suspending power had been condemned outright, and the dispensing power as it had been used of late, but there was no suggestion that the people were framing a new form of government for themselves. Rather, they had acted to defend an inherited tradition against the aggressions of a foolish and irresponsible monarch.

Having established the extent to which Price had erred in his treatment of 1689 Burke turned his attention to the contrast between the English Revolution and what was happening in France. Like all of his works, his *Reflections on the Revolution in France* was the product of a particular political crisis. Burke's broader and more philosophical generalisations stemmed from the needs of the situation to which he was addressing himself. Burke rooted everything he said in what was essentially an historical treatment of his subject. Tradition explained the success of the Glorious Revolution in England. The English had not forgotten the legacy of the past; rather they had treasured it. Change might be forced upon them, but it would be constructive and truly improving only if it were organically related to the previous experience of the nation shown down the centuries. It was impossible to tear up the past and start afresh; it was a sure recipe for disaster rashly and arrogantly to attempt to do so.

Burke attempted to draw analogies between Britain and France in such a way as to suggest an alternative to what was happening. Here his ignorance of much of what had taken place in France, and the ease with which he accepted at face value much of what he had been told by émigrés and enemies of the Revolution, often led him astray. He exaggerated the potentialities for reform under the *ancien régime*. He mistook the nature of the French *parlements*, overlooking their character as privileged legal corporations rather than representative institutions. He romanticised the French monarchy, as the famous passage rhapsodising over the beauty of Marie Antoinette and the passing of the age of chivalry flamboyantly revealed. But despite the glaring flaws in much of what he said about French institutions and the nature of French society Burke elevated the debate to a new level and introduced a profundity of insight, a breadth of vision, and a sense of high tragedy which had been wholly lacking in previous British responses to events in France.

In many ways his perception was uncanny. Long before there seemed any obvious danger of any form of dictatorship in France Burke affirmed that the Revolution's greatest driving force was its tendency towards centralisation. He saw it as totalitarianism masquerading in liberal dress. He forecast that the ideology of revolution would soon approximate to a secular religion. This would lead to intolerance, persecution, a denial of fundamental freedoms, and ultimately an assault upon Christianity. The centralising tendency of the Revolution would destroy liberty in France. Civil war would follow. As well as plunging France into confusion and bloodshed, the ideology of revolution would threaten the peace and stability of all Europe. Burke discerned a messianic element in the Revolution which would generate war and military dictatorship. Having destroyed every familiar institution, every focus of loyalty which stood between the individual and the state, the revolutionaries would have to resort to the army as the only force capable of restoring order. As a convinced Christian Burke saw the Revolution as a secular, atheistic religion, and the war engendered by the Revolution would be more terrible than the old wars of religion. It would be a war of righteousness, relentless in its ferocity, appalling and catastrophic in its effects. What was happening in France transcended the mere reordering of French institutions. It posed a threat to traditional institutions in Europe, both civil and religious, and it was therefore the concern of every responsible statesman to recognise the threat of the French Revolution, with all that it implied by way of anarchy, violence and conflict, and to take action to crush the monster before the whole of Christendom was plunged into strife. Burke's critics saw this as alarmism, an eccentric demand for intervention in France on the basis of a lurid overreaction to events.

When Burke's book was published in November 1790 it provoked a great debate. In retrospect it might appear that every thoughtful Englishman must have acted on George III's advice – that Mr Burke's book was one which every gentleman should read. But many of the initial reactions to Burke's intervention were hostile. Before the Flight to Varennes in June 1791 much of what Burke said seemed unduly pessimistic. Many replies purporting to refute Burke's book were published, the most intellectually adroit being Mackintosh's *Vindiciae Gallicae*, the most popular and effervescent being Paine's *Rights of Man*. But radicals and reformers were not the only people unhappy or uneasy about Burke's call for intervention. Pitt had no desire to be dragged into the complications of French politics, whatever Burke's warnings demanded of him. He still believed that British interests would be best served by a policy of strict neutrality. There is no truth in old legends that Pitt's gold corrupted the French National Assembly, luring the French from one blunder to another with the subtle intent of reducing Britain's greatest rival to a state of impotence. Such tales were propagated by French revolutionaries eager to see Pitt's hand in everything and to exonerate the Revolution from the charge that it was foredoomed to violence. When Burke and Pitt dined together in the summer of 1791 Burke was depressed by Pitt's complacency. 'Depend upon it, Mr Burke,' Pitt had said, 'we shall go on as we are to the Day of Judgement.' Burke replied that it was the day of no judgement he was afraid of. It seemed to him that the government regarded French affairs with a narrow-minded detachment which boded ill for the future. Burke wanted to alert the ministers into seeing that they were faced with a major crisis, a threat to everything achieved in Britain since the ejection of James II. But then Burke had always thought Pitt lacking in vision. He had often seen him as a shallow and unscrupulous opportunist, concerned only with perpetuating his own tenure of office. Sadly, Burke believed that the British political scene was dominated by opportunists, men who were devoid of any profundity or insight, and who were willing to sacrifice almost every principle to the attainment of place and the enjoyment of all the perquisites of public life. He came to believe that the ideology of revolution made a peculiar appeal to desperate and ruined men, who would seek to rebuild their own fortunes on the wreck of public happiness.

Burke's relationship with the Foxite party was also under strain. He had long felt excluded, isolated, ignored, misunderstood and wilfully misrepresented by those who prided themselves on their Whig principles while showing no compunction about shedding them when immediate advantages were in the offing. The challenge of the French Revolution made Burke all the more convinced that the younger Foxites were willing to flirt with dangerous ideas in their desperate search for political advancement. Fox had praised the French and rejoiced in the sack of the Bastille. That had been bad but the behaviour of Sheridan and Grey had been worse. They went out of their way to endorse what was going on in France and to provoke Burke, both inside the House of Commons and outside it. They were eager to use the French Revolution as the occasion for the restoration of links with radicals and reformers which had been broken by the events of the previous five years. Burke responded by seeking to convince the more conservative Foxites, such as Portland and Fitzwilliam, that the French Revolution raised issues which made the squabbles between Pittite and Foxite trivial and irrelevant. The French Revolution challenged the English constitution, threatened property, and substituted abstract principle for that respect for tradition which had been the secret of Whig achievements in Britain. Some members of the opposition were already sympathetic to Burke's ideas. Windham was a ready listener and Loughborough likewise was uneasy about the French Revolution. Both Burke and Loughborough had felt betrayed by their colleagues during the Regency Crisis; now their misgivings were intensified by a controversy which raised more fundamental questions. Nevertheless, Burke encountered much frustration during 1790 and 1791. The ministers seemed lethargic in their response to his warnings and the conservative Whigs were slow to rise to the challenge of events.

Portland was hesitant because he had no desire to jeopardise the future of the Foxite party. Ominous though developments in France were it was foolish to allow French affairs to dominate British political debate. To permit this to happen would be the surest way of giving Pitt the opportunity to divide and destroy the opposition. Whatever their fears about French ideas and the French example, Portland and Fitzwilliam had no wish to do anything which would play into the hands of their hated and feared adversary. Similarly, Fox was all too conscious of the strains and stresses within the ranks of his followers. Emotionally he shared much of the enthusiasm of his younger friends for the principles, though not always the practice, of the French reformers. Rationally Fox was aware of the dangers of committing the party to an extreme pro-French stance. He knew that hostility to the French was an ingrained characteristic of British political life. If the French reformers mishandled their attempts to establish a constitutional monarchy in France sympathy in Britain would easily turn to enmity. Fox's greatest preoccupation was the preservation of the identity of the opposition Whig party. If things went well in France – and Fox was reluctant to abandon hopes of a happy outcome – then the controversy provoked by Burke would cease to have any political significance. It would be relegated to the obscurity of ephemeral intellectual debate and would cease to have any political importance. Fox sought, therefore, to encourage the younger members of his party by appearing sympathetic to using the French situation to regenerate the reform movement under Whig patronage, while at the same time damping down the fears of Portland and Fitzwilliam by keeping alive their suspicions of Pitt. In private Fox tried to persuade his colleagues to drop the practice of goading Burke.

The problem was that in 1790 and 1791 debates over issues such as Nootka Sound and Pitt's Canada Bill kept French controversies in the public eye. Nootka Sound allowed pro-French sympathisers to point to the denunciation of the old Family Compact between the French and Spanish Bourbons as evidence that the French reformers were acting up to their protestations of peace and their renunciation of dynastic ambitions. Most British commentators ignored the extent to which attitudes within the French National Assembly had been determined by desires to limit the powers of the crown or assert the authority of the Assembly, rather than by any friendship towards Britain, but the refusal of the French to support the Spaniards contributed to Britain's diplomatic victory in the dispute. The Canada Bill posed more difficult problems. Because it proposed dividing Canada into two provinces, Upper and Lower Canada, and because it involved making special provisions for the welfare of French Canadians and the security of the Catholic church in Quebec, it tempted politicians to draw all sorts of analogies between Pitt's reform of government in Canada and the reforms which were being promulgated in the French National Assembly.

The debate on the Canada Bill brought the relationship between Burke and Fox to crisis-point. They had long acted together in politics since the days when, stage by stage, Fox had allied himself with the Rockinghamites during the American War. They were publicly associated with a number of issues: economical reform, the attack on crown influence, the defence of party, reforms in India and Ireland. But they had never been as close personally as many assumed. Burke was averse to the mode of life connected with the Prince of Wales and he had never shared Fox's raffish lifestyle. After the fiasco of the India Bill and the downfall of the Fox-North coalition, Burke had felt excluded from the councils of the party. The Regency Crisis had compounded his feelings of rejection. These were now heightened by the debate over the French Revolution and particularly by the conduct of Grey and Sheridan in the House of Commons. In April 1791 Fox and Burke met to reconcile their differences. All seemed to go well. The old campaigners walked down to the House of Commons arm in arm. But in May 1791, during a debate on the Canada Bill, Burke was so outraged by the more radical Foxites that he urged his friends to flee from the French Revolution. In considerable distress Fox interjected that he hoped there would be no loss of friends. Burke replied that he was sacrificing his friendships to the great cause of saving civilisation from the Revolution. Fox was brokenhearted. Whatever their differences he had never wanted their association to end in public recrimination. Though some of the Foxites were relieved that Burke had broken his tenuous links with the party, Fox knew that the loss of Burke would put even greater strain on Portland and Fitzwilliam and that this would heighten the danger of further leakage from the opposition.

Reform Movements

There were other anxieties pressing upon the opposition at this time. The French Revolution had revitalised the rather moribund popular reform movement in Britain. As we have seen, the success of Pitt's peacetime administration had so restored confidence in the system that it was hard for those eager to reform parliament or to repeal the Test and Corporation Acts to make much impact on the public. The dramatic events in France had given them new heart. The Society for Constitutional Information became active again. Now that the French were imitating the English it was timely for England to imitate France. Fox and his friends were in a predicament. They were bitterly aware of the extent to which Pitt had seized the initiative in bidding for popular support during the King's illness. Now that reform was in the air there was a possibility of turning the tables on Pitt and regaining the confidence of those who had moved away from the Foxites since 1783. But to achieve this would not be simple. The range of opinion among the popular reformers was wide. Some, such as Christopher Wyvill, represented the familiar moderate approach, with an emphasis on a redistribution of parliamentary constituencies, an increase in county representation, and possibly a return to triennial parliaments. Others, fired by the French example and excited by the oratory of Richard Price, were attracted to more radical solutions. They talked of household suffrage, even of votes for all adult males, and annual parliaments. It was difficult to know how to appeal to popular reformers without frightening Portland and Fitzwilliam and their friends. The Rockinghamites and Foxites had never been of one mind on parliamentary reform. It had always been an open question, whether in office or opposition. To support demands even for a moderate reform of parliament too vocally would embarrass and antagonise Portland still further. Yet Fox, Grey and Sheridan were also aware that if the party made no bid for popular support there was a danger that the leadership of the reform movement would fall into the hands of radical extremists. The result would then be that Fox would be rejected by radicals as well as by conservatives.

It was not surprising, therefore, that Fox found it hard to know how to maintain a semblance of party unity when there were so many pressures tearing the party apart. It was this understandable uncertainty which explained much of the confusion surrounding the formation of the Society of the Friends of the People in 1792. Grey and Sheridan were convinced that by setting up the Society under the aegis of their party they would be able to snatch the initiative in the reform debate, outwit the advanced radicals, and control the mainstream of reformist opinion. They would then be in an excellent position to exploit the situation by contrasting Pitt's commitment to reform in 1785 with his reluctance to consider a reform of parliament in the 1790s. In later life, when he was seeking to distance himself from the radicalism of his youth, Grey claimed that one word from Fox would have saved him from all the nonsense of the Friends of the People. But Fox had urged caution, only to have his warnings spurned. He lamented that his friends seemed determined to take no advice, and especially not to take his. The year 1792 saw, not a happy resolution of the French crisis, but a remarkable deterioration in French affairs. In the spring the Brissotin government went to war with Austria and Prussia. The French met early reverses in the field. The result was the revolution of 10 August, which led to the fall of the French monarchy, the declaration of a republic, the horrors of the September massacres, and the onset of terror and dictatorship.

Yet, even without such a dramatic confirmation of Burke's prognosis the Foxites would have found it hard to maintain control of popular reform movements. One new feature of the situation was that artisans were beginning to organise radical societies for themselves, without relying on men such as Wyvill, Horne Tooke or Grey, or accepting what they thought was a suitable provision for reform. Many advanced radicals sent good wishes to the French National Assembly. This, and the goodwill extended to the French convention after the fall of the monarchy, strengthened suspicions that the reform movement in England was falling ominously under the sway of French-style extremists. In London, Thomas Hardy, a shoemaker and committed reformer, was prominent in setting up the London Corresponding Society. The Society advocated a programme of radical parliamentary reform: universal male suffrage, the abolition of the property qualification for MPs, equal electoral districts, the payment of MPs, annual parliaments, the secret ballot. The Society was as democratic in its organisation as in its objectives. It was an artisan society and it sought to coordinate the parliamentary reform movement throughout the country by means of correspondence. It was its artisan character and its aspiration to establish the popular reform movement on a more permanent and better organised basis which made it seem so sinister to so many members of the political nation. Men such as Hardy were no longer willing to defer to the leadership of charitably disposed Whigs. And despite its name the Society of the Friends of the People was an unrepentantly aristocratic society. It represented a commitment to household suffrage and to redistribution, but it was intended to control the popular reform movement as much as to invigorate it. Faced with the competition of the London Corresponding Society the action of Grey and Sheridan in founding the Friends of the People was unlikely to achieve its objective, but it nevertheless intensified the suspicions felt by conservatives, whether within the Foxite group or outside it. The 1790s saw a revival of popular political awareness, but although this seemed initially to benefit the cause of reform, the deteriorating situation in Europe and fears about possible French interference in the domestic politics of Britain meant that the popular consciousness swung violently and enthusiastically behind loyalism. The greatest shift of political feeling in the 1790s was the eruption of patriotic loyalism, staunchly opposed to anything savouring of French ideas and committed, especially after Britain found herself at war with France, to resisting French republicanism by force of arms and refuting Jacobin ideology both by argument and action.

Pitt came under pressure in two ways. First, there were those such as Burke who wanted the government to be more forthright in challenging and resisting the French Revolution, and secondly there were those who demanded stricter securities against domestic radicalism, since any threat to British institutions and property was a greater worry than the fate of the French monarchy. Pitt knew how important it was to respond to opinion among the backbenchers in the House of Commons. He was also conscious of the tensions within the Foxite opposition. If he were to tempt Portland or Fitzwilliam to break with Fox he would have to be sensitive towards their anxieties and preoccupations. Portland and the opposition conservatives did not view the French Revolution purely as a foreign event. With considerable estates in Yorkshire and Derbyshire, aristocrats such as Portland, Fitzwilliam and Devonshire were fully cognisant of the fact that Sheffield was a centre of radicalism. Demands for manhood suffrage, the ballot and annual parliaments went far beyond what any conservative could contemplate, and demands for change looked all the more threatening when they were associated with an ideology derived from Jacobinism. By the summer of 1792 it was clear that the ideals of 1789 were being overtaken by an ideology which owed more to Rousseau than to Montesquieu, and which was more closely related to the desire of the French to win the war than a disinterested longing to elevate the lot of humanity. With hindsight it is possible to see that the majority of British radicals were reformers, not Jacobins. However advanced their thinking or their schemes of reform they had little in common with the French Jacobins, but for contemporaries such distinctions were blurred by the passion of debate and the fury of events.

Problems for Pitt

Pitt had other anxieties as well as the complications created by divisions within the ranks of the opposition. In 1791 he had lost his foreign secretary, the Duke of Leeds. Leeds was bitterly disappointed by Pitt's failure to maintain a forward policy in the Near East. The attempt to challenge Russian expansion in the Black Sea region had failed. Urged on by his

Prussian allies Pitt had initially opposed the actions of the Empress Catherine, but because of divisions within the cabinet, unease in the naval high command, the loss of support in the Commons, and conflicting assessments of Prussian motivation, Pitt had to climb down over the Orchakov affair. The weaknesses of the Triple Alliance had been cruelly exposed. The opposition had succeeded in embarrassing Pitt over Orchakov. For a time they believed themselves to be on the brink of overthrowing the government. Pitt extricated himself, but Leeds resented what he considered weakness on Pitt's part. When Leeds resigned as foreign secretary Pitt promoted his cousin, W. W. Grenville, to the vacant post. Other ministerial changes followed. In the spring of 1792 Thurlow indicated that he intended to challenge the government's fiscal policies in the Lords. For the lord chancellor to take such action transgressed the liberal standards of collective responsibility accepted by members of the cabinet. There were issues – parliamentary reform, the slave trade, religious disabilities – on which the lord chancellor might legitimately have distanced himself from the prime minister of the day, but governments were expected to approach financial questions with an agreed mind. Pitt was able to compel Thurlow to resign. Their relations had been cool ever since Thurlow's deviousness in 1788. But Thurlow's departure came at a difficult time. There was no obvious successor as lord chancellor. The Great Seal was put in commission, though this could only be a temporary expedient. But there was one candidate for the lord chancellorship who was eager to thrust himself forward. Loughborough had never forgotten nor forgiven the slights he had endured from his colleagues during the Regency crisis. Since then he had taken a strongly critical line over the French Revolution and the response of the Foxites to events in France. He did not, however, wish to be seen as acting alone. He sought to set in motion a negotiation to broaden the scope of Pitt's ministry by bringing in those members of the opposition who were so perturbed by the French Revolution and the dangers of domestic radicalism as to accept the need to forget old enmities and establish a national coalition strong enough to face the Jacobin challenge at home and abroad.

Pitt was sceptical of the likelihood of such a negotiation succeeding. Whatever their embarrassments and anxieties Pitt suspected that most of the Foxites were not yet ready to sever their connection with Fox. As for Fox, he was struggling hard to prevent the disruption of his party. Pitt thought it unlikely that Fox would swallow his pride and accept office. But the negotiation was worth trying. It would show Loughborough that Pitt was sensitive about his situation and it would be a valuable goodwill gesture. It would also put additional pressure upon the more conservative Foxites. If it succeeded, Pitt would have the satisfaction of presiding over a government which met the conventional demands of constitutional theory: his administration would clearly be one which transcended party loyalties, dissolved familiar factions, and rallied patriotic opinion to the defence of the nation. If it failed, it would add to the problems of the opposition and would make the Foxites appear churlish, partisan, and so narrow-minded as to be unable to view events in national, rather than party, terms. Pitt was shrewd enough to be fair in what he offered the opposition by way of appointments, but he was not surprised when Fox killed off the chances of a positive outcome by stating that while he would serve with Pitt he would not serve under him. Fox attempted to win back the trust of Portland by suggesting that Portland should head a new administration, with Pitt and himself working under him, perhaps as secretaries of state. Fox knew that such a suggestion was wholly unacceptable to Pitt. It was a repetition of his old tactic of blocking a negotiation without appearing too crudely to reject it.

Loughborough was disappointed at the response of his erstwhile colleagues, but he felt free to accept the lord chancellorship. Portland and Fitzwilliam could not bring themselves to abandon Fox, although they were increasingly gloomy about the French situation. But they thought that acquiescing in the dissolution of their party was too high a price to pay for a measure of additional security against Jacobinism. It was still possible that the European war would end quickly. This would resolve the French problem and allow British politics to get back to what both conservative and liberal Foxites liked to think of as normality. But while Portland hoped that the French would lose the war Fox could not disguise his own desire for a French victory. He detested the actions of the absolutist powers in Poland and he affirmed that the excesses of the French revolutionaries, abhorrent as they were, had been provoked by the behaviour of the royalists and their allies. The Duke of Brunswick's manifesto was an outrageous interference in the internal affairs of France and it had set in train the very developments the émigrés had hoped to avert. Fox was depressed and gloomy. For much of the time he tried to identify at least one group in France which was equivalent to the English Whigs. Again and again the various French factions disappointed his expectations. He knew little of the French political scene. He acted on guesswork, speculation and wishful thinking. His humanitarian instincts were appalled by the September massacres; his liberal conscience was offended by Brunswick's manifesto. Amid so much uncertainty the only sane move was to preserve, at all costs, the opposition party in England. It would be nothing less than tragic if over-reactions to the French Revolution permitted Pitt to destroy the one group in politics which was staunchly opposed to him. Hostility to Pitt was virtually the only attitude on which the opposition could agree. Although Portland and the other conservatives wanted the government to take firm action to curb English radicalism and to check the spread of Jacobinism, they came to the conclusion that the crisis did not, as yet, justify abandoning Fox and throwing in their lot with Pitt. Fox had worked hard to save this much from the wreck. He was bitter, blaming Burke for subverting the loyalty of members of the party and conspiring to create a coalition government committed to an interventionist stance in Europe. Yet, in his more dejected moments, Fox could confess that Burke was right but that he had been right too soon. Unsatisfactory as it was for all parties, 1792 failed to see a resolution of the major issue of when and how a realignment of political forces would take place.

While Pitt coolly sought to exploit the anguish of his opponents, he had no wish to depart from his policy of neutrality and peace. In February 1792, in his famous speech surveying the financial policies of the government, Pitt had conceded that a long period of peace was necessary if his fiscal and commercial initiatives were to ripen. He went so far as to suggest that there had never been a time when the omens for a prolonged peace in Europe were so promising, committing himself to the hazardous forecast of fifteen years. He was too experienced a politician not to hedge his estimate with qualifications about the uncertainty of peering into the future, but most people remembered his optimism and forgot his reservations. However blighted by events the speech demonstrated the depth of Pitt's commitment to peace. This set him apart from those who were urging Britain to join in a grand coalition to crush Jacobinism once and for all. Burke affirmed that the greatest challenge facing the rulers of Europe was the threat of Jacobinism; the ideology of Jacobinism was even more menacing than the military power of the French republic. Pitt did not share such assumptions. His mind moved in more mundane and less speculative realms. The two men closest to him, Dundas and Grenville, endorsed Pitt's standpoint. Dundas, a realistic and observant politician, was always sceptical about overbold gestures, and Grenville, although later amenable to a grand strategy which went far beyond what Dundas thought practicable, was just as committed to cautious neutrality. In the autumn of 1792 Grenville told his brother,

Buckingham, of the importance of keeping aloof from foreign entangle-ments while seeking to do whatever was possible to ease the lot of the British people and damp down the enthusiasm of the radicals. The ministers faced a growing groundswell of opinion which was alarmed by the activities of radicals and which saw British radicals as the dupes or agents of the French.

Paine and Radicalism

Fears of a French-inspired conspiracy were heightened by the tendency of some radicals to talk in language reminiscent of French extremism rather than of British self-control. The year 1792 saw the transformation of the radical movement in Britain. While many reformers lamented the swing to the right, the upsurge of loyalism was given additional impetus by the initiative taken by John Reeves in founding constitutionalist associations. The more cautious reformers began to draw back from anything tainted with republicanism or fondness for the French cause. But others came to redefine their position in ways which made it more challenging and more extreme, and from the point of view of the polit-ical nation, more ominous. Wyvill had always said that nothing would damage the cause of intelligent reform more than the conduct of radical extremists. His fears were justified by events. Some radicals, particularly those who were devout Dissenters, had been shocked by the atheism of many of the more vociferous French revolutionaries. They had rejoiced at attacks on the privileges of the Catholic church in France but they felt horror and outrage at the desecration of churches, the persecution of priests and nuns, and the attempt to dechristianise France. They affirmed their loyalty to the ideals of 1789 but distanced themselves from the ferocity of the regime in Paris. But while many reformers were fearful of the consequences of confusing reform with revolution, and timely improvement with chaos, others accepted in full the provocative ideology of Thomas Paine, whose book *Rights of Man* was easily the most popular reply to Burke's *Reflections*.

Paine cheerfully denounced the anomalies of the English constitution, comparing it unfavourably with the French constitution of 1791. He offended many Englishmen – Fox among them – by the disrespect with which he treated British institutions. His comments on the defects of the hereditary principle, or the vagaries of the franchise in England, or the role of aristocracy were amusing, irreverent, memorable, and to traditionalist Whigs or old-fashioned reformers, shocking and deeply disturbing. Even worse was his advocacy of a redistributive income tax and a system of welfare benefits. His disrespect for monarchy was matched only by his apparent disrespect for property. Even more sensational was the boldness with which he asserted a philosophy based on natural rights. Although Paine made ample use of the old legends about Magna Carta and the Norman Yoke which had long provided English radicalism with its own fanciful version of history and a validation of its claim to be doing no more than seeking a return to a purer and more democratic past, he insisted that the true rights of man were those indicated by nature and reason and available to all men everywhere, regardless of local culture or varying traditions. The notion that all men had inherent political and civil rights was an advanced and revolutionary proposal in the 1790s. Many English reformers still preferred to ground their schemes of reform on ideas of purification, the restoration of the balance of the constitution, the recognition of new forms of property. While the number of radicals faithful to the demand for immediate and sweeping reform declined because of the distorting impact of developments in France upon the national consciousness, those who remained faithful to the cause of advanced reform were now more likely to be Painite in their ideology. Radicalism became the creed of a shrinking minority, but it became tougher, better-integrated, and more profoundly challenging to traditional modes of thinking about the political system. Paine's imprisonment in Paris during the reign of terror heightened the prevalence of the feeling that the French had lost their way and that they had betrayed the ideals of 1789. But it did not weaken the grip of Painite ideology upon the thinking of the small band of faithful radicals, especially those from an artisan background. Paine articulated the grievances and aspirations of many shopkeepers and craftsmen, men who prided themselves on their thrift and independence and who were now impatient and angry over their exclusion from the political nation. Although Jeremy Bentham was to provide radicalism with another ideology, condemning the French Declaration of the Rights of Man as nonsense on stilts, Paine gave radical artisans and tradesmen a distinctive voice.

But while advanced radicalism became more Painite many contemporaries saw it as the child of Jacobinism, the offspring of the French Revolution. This was to ignore those traditions within radicalism which went back to the seventeenth century. Although radicalism had been given additional impetus by the French Revolution, its roots were firmly English. Yet even here attempts to invoke memories of the Civil War and Interregnum were counterproductive. The excesses of the Levellers and Diggers, the sectarian disputes of the Protectorate, the rule of Cromwell and the major-generals, were more likely to inspire fierce conservatism than engender a more vital radicalism. Both radicals and conservatives fell victim to wishful thinking. This failing was compounded by the French. When the Convention passed the Edict of Fraternity, promising French help to all peoples struggling to throw off oppression, and when the French minister of marine talked of sending 50 000 caps of liberty to England, suspicions that there was a deep-laid Jacobin plot to subvert the country's institutions seemed to be confirmed. In the closing months of December 1792 there were rumours of an insurrection planned for December, to take place in London. Pitt was sceptical about the so-called December insurrection, but he felt it wise to take precautions. When the rising failed to take place, Pitt's scepticism was amply justified, but he saw how necessary it was to take note of the fears and anxieties rampant in the nation. He was also poised to make the most of new opportunities of exploiting the difficulties of the opposition.

Britain at War

British opinion was horrified by the execution of Louis XVI – not even Tom Paine could convince the Convention to show mercy to the King – but Pitt was much more worried by French designs on the Low Countries and the unilateral denunciation of international treaty obligations than by the savagery of French domestic politics. On 1 February 1793, the French Convention declared war on Britain. To the last Pitt had obdurately hoped for peace. Although after the fall of the French monarchy in August 1792 Pitt had refrained from recognising the French republic, and although he had recalled Lord Gower, the British ambassador, from Paris he had sought to maintain unofficial links with the French government. His own preference was for a constitutional monarchy in France, but if the republic could win the confidence of the majority of Frenchmen, show that it could rule effectively, and continue to honour France's treaty obligations, Pitt did not rule out ultimate recognition. But, once the two countries were at war, both sides discerned a certain inevitability about events. Pitt refused to fight the war primarily for the restoration of the Bourbons, but the exigencies of the war compelled him to aid French royalists who were resisting the republic. His chief aims were to check French aggression in Europe, restore traditional frontiers, and reaffirm the binding power of international treaties, but although the British government never subscribed to the ideological view of the war expounded with tenacious eloquence and fiery imagination by Burke, it was impossible in such a conflict to maintain an absolute and logical distinction between a clash of interests and a war of ideologies.

Virtually nobody in England – with the possible exception of Burke – expected the war to be other than short. It seemed impossible that the French republic, its army already weakened by the emigration of many of its officers, should be able to withstand the combined strength of Austria, Prussia and Britain. But no one anticipated the brilliance and determination with which the French improvised a new army and a new method of waging war. They defeated the armies of the *ancien régime* because they refused to abide by the familiar conventions of formal warfare. Soon the French were able, not only to deny victory to the invaders of their country, but to take the war into neighbouring territories. Invasion was cloaked with the ideology of liberation. Another of Burke's prophecies had come true: the French now set up satellite regimes wherever their armies triumphed. At first, during his protracted efforts to keep out of the war, Pitt had conceded that in their fight against the Austrians the French would inevitably campaign in Flanders. He had refused to panic about this. But once the French rejected the legitimacy of those regimes whose territory they had invaded, taking the opportunity conferred by victory to make permanent changes in the domestic institutions of the Netherlands, the war took on a dimension which boded ill for hopes of a speedy termination of hostilities.

Once Britain was immersed in war, public opinion tolerated nothing which smacked, however remotely, of Jacobinism. As the war dragged on, and as the fortunes of war tilted in favour of the French, fears of domestic upheaval, supposedly masterminded by traitors and enemy agents, became inflamed and widespread. The government was called upon to preserve domestic tranquillity as well as to wage war by land and sea. Stage by stage the ministry reacted to these demands, but the Portland Whigs felt that Pitt's response was too tardy, too inclined merely to follow the course of untoward events. When it became obvious that there was not going to be a speedy end to the war Portland and his friends reluctantly recognised that if the war was to be won and the threat of Jacobinism, whether domestic or foreign, dispelled then a coalition with Pitt was inescapable. In their hearts they did not desire it; to the end they hoped that some change of fortune might save them from taking the dreaded and decisive step. But the behaviour of Fox, Sheridan and Grey had only multiplied the anxieties of their more conservative colleagues, and after a period of negotiation Portland and his group joined the government in July 1794. For two years they had agonised over the necessity of breaking with Fox. Now Portland became home secretary, and was therefore responsible for whatever action was needed to halt the inroads of radicalism and Jacobinism. Fitzwilliam became lord president of the council, and then in December 1794 lord lieutenant of Ireland. Dundas became war secretary; Grenville continued as foreign secretary. In parliamentary strength the new coalition was invincible. Fox's following shrank to a mere 60 MPs, only about half of whom were committed to the cause of parliamentary reform. Those who continued to support Fox did so because they shared his misgivings over the war or because they found the pull of his personality more powerful than their political uncertainties.

What Burke and Loughborough had desired in 1792 had now come about, but it had needed a war to bring into being a ministry formed on the broadest possible basis, with an equitable distribution of posts among the various groups belonging to it. Despite the pressure of events Pitt remained prime minister. There was never any likelihood that he would step down. His dominance appeared more formidable than ever, even when old foes accepted that they were compelled by necessity rather than choice to acquiesce in his leadership. The two colleagues, Dundas and Grenville, who more than any others possessed his confidence, remained of crucial importance in determining the main thrust of government policy. Furthermore, Pitt still retained the trust of George III. He was the King's preference as chief minister, and the knowledge that Pitt remained the King's choice persuaded the majority of MPs that even when the ministry was reshuffled to accommodate the Portland Whigs, they could continue to feel that Pitt was in command, secure in the affections of his sovereign and dominant within the councils of the state.

The coalition of 1794 marked the ruin of Fox's hopes. The opposition had, after all, broken up. Pitt's ability to turn even crisis into an opportunity to tighten his grip on power loomed over every other facet of the political scene. It seemed that there was nothing except loyalty to Fox left to hold the tiny opposition group together. Grey had raised the issue of parliamentary reform in 1792 and 1793 to little effect and to some embarrassment. Fox and Grey had disagreed in 1792 about the wisdom of raising the question of reform. Fox had argued that it would only antagonise the Portland group and make their desertion to Pitt more likely. When Grey persisted, Fox had felt compelled by loyalty and friendship to support him in the Commons, despite his misgivings. Neither Fox nor Grey wished to endorse the radical demands associated with the London Corresponding Society. But parliamentary reform had been overshadowed by fears of Jacobinism, and after the departure of the Portland Whigs the Foxites sought to challenge the government over the conduct of the war and the means by which the ministry was combating radicalism.

Fox had always been devoted to civil and religious liberty. He deplored religious tests for public office and anything which limited the rights of the subject in matters such as free speech, public assembly, and petitioning the crown. When the government tightened up the law controlling the admission of aliens into the country Fox had been incensed. Even more upsetting were the treason trials, when radicals in England and Scotland were charged with high treason rather than mere seditious libel. Fox was justifiably outraged by the conduct of the trials in Scotland, where Lord Braxfield presided over the trials of Muir and Palmer without any pretence of objectivity. But in England, Horne Tooke, Thelwall and Thomas Hardy were acquitted on charges of treason. Had the government proceeded on lesser charges, convictions might have been secured, but the embarrassment of acquittals was worth risking because the ministers had calculated that the deterrent effect of charges of treason would be greater than that of convictions for sedition. The consequences of the trials proved them right. Radical activity declined. When popular demonstrations occurred these were inspired by food shortages and rising prices, not a desire for a reform of parliament. When the ministry passed the Seditious Meetings and Treasonable Practices Acts, which gave magistrates additional powers in restricting public meetings, Fox's anger was boundless. He talked as if Pitt and Portland were mounting an assault upon the fundamental liberties of the subject. That his old colleague Portland was particularly active as home secretary in the effort to restrain radical activism only made Fox more irritable.

But Pitt and Portland did not preside over anything like a reign of terror. Something like a total of 200 prosecutions over a period of ten years hardly merits such a description. Many of the cases ended in acquittal or in the charges being quietly dropped and the proceedings discontinued. The pressure of convention and the weight of public opinion achieved more in damping down radicalism than either the Seditious Meetings Act or the Treasonable Practices Act. With the ascendancy of loyalism and the popular identification of radicalism with Jacobinism, radicals suffered more from the prejudices of the community than from the force of law. There was never any truth in the suggestion that England was populated by fearsome radical extremists who were longing to rise in arms in collaboration with the French (though passions were rather different in Ireland). As long as the country was threatened by invasion – and this danger seemed all the greater when Britain stood alone after Austria made peace with France in 1797 – the London Corresponding Society affirmed that its members would play their part in resisting the French should they land an army in England. Even the radical subjects of George III shared their sovereign's determination that if the enemy landed they would proceed towards him in order to drive him into the sea. If the period was a period of repression, this was brought about by a movement of public opinion rather than being imposed from above. There has been much vigorous and controversial debate about the nature of radicalism, the likelihood of revolution, and the strength of the revolutionary element within the radical movement, but most historians would see radicalism as essentially law-abiding and constitutionalist, with only a tiny fringe of extremists being devoted to violence rather than persuasion as the means of achieving reform. Men such as Thomas Hardy, who were committed to a genuinely democratic reform of the political system, remained loyal to their belief that agitation should be within the law. The British radicals shared several characteristics with the French Jacobins: many of them were artisans, small shopkeepers, independent tradesmen or skilled craftsmen. There the similarity ended. While French reformers were compelled to see their chief function as that of trying to transform a speculative ideal into a reality, English radicals were preoccupied with restoring purity to a system which had a long history of continuity, however much it might have decayed. There was, therefore, a greater concern for the practicalities of politics even among advanced radicals. Those who retained some regard for the ideals of 1789 interpreted them in the light of the English, not the French, experience. Under the directory and consulate many English radicals felt that the French republic had been betrayed, the rulers of France frustrating rather than fulfilling the dreams of 1789. A firm distinction came to be made between the ideals of the Revolution and the hideous conduct of those who ruled France. Robespierre was denounced as a bloodthirsty tyrant, the Directory as corrupt, Bonaparte as no more than a French Cromwell. It was hard, indeed virtually impossible, to differentiate controversies over domestic reform from attitudes to the war. The majority of Englishmen placed loyalty to the crown and fidelity to the constitution above anything which could be deemed sympathetic to the French.

Thus, when Britain stood alone, there was little comfort for Fox and his tiny band of supporters. In the late 1790s Fox and his friends were so depressed by the political prospect that they seceded from the House of Commons. Secession was another reversion to an outmoded and backward-looking political tactic. It signalled the depths of frustration to which the Foxite opposition had sunk. They knew that they had little chance of shaking Pitt's majorities, however badly the war went, and they knew that even if Pitt were discredited, the King would not turn to Fox to replace him. The central fact of the continued importance of the prerogative of the crown remained an immovable obstacle in Fox's path. In 1795 and 1796 there were abortive attempts to reach a negotiated peace with the French. Pitt did not rule out a peace if the right terms could be agreed. This exposed much of what Fox had said about Pitt wantonly throwing away chance after chance of peace as irresponsible and inaccurate. The failure of the negotiations left most Englishmen convinced that the responsibility for the continuation of the war lay where it had always lain, with the French.

Yet Fox's criticism of the war had seen him at his most eloquent in calling for a limited war for limited objectives. He was defending the traditional eighteenth-century concept of war for verifiable objectives. In one sense he was fighting an irrelevant contest, since Pitt had never subscribed to the ideological view of the war expounded by Burke. But, however persuasive much of Fox's rhetoric was, his motives were not wholly idealistic. Much of his conduct during the war years stemmed from a fundamental miscalculation as to what would happen if the war went badly for Britain. Fox believed that if the war led to defeat or stalemate Pitt would suffer from a withdrawal of confidence similar to that which had finally forced North to resign towards the close of the war in America. But the French war posed more immediate threats to the nation than the American War had done. Pitt and the government could credibly depict the present war as a struggle for survival, Jacobinism constituting a threat to the English constitution and the British way of life. Fox's analogy with the American War, like many analogies indulged in for political effect, was defective and inadequate. More significant than any similarities between the American and French wars were the immense differences between them. Fox's miscalculation could not be redeemed by oratory. Just as in the 1780s the opposition had been compelled to fall back upon a reliance upon the Prince of Wales, with disastrous consequences, so in the 1790s the failure of the attempt to exploit the war as a means of discrediting Pitt forced Fox to fall back upon another obsolete tactic, that of secession from the House of Commons.

The party which was still committed, at least in principle, to the reduction of the powers of the crown, the enlargement of the collective responsibilities of the cabinet to cover both policy and the choice of a first minister, and the acceptance of party and formed opposition, was driven by the relentless pressure of events to fall back on tactics which contradicted the innovations for which they were pleading. The Foxites could not match rhetoric with action. Their theory of politics remained remote from much of their practice. Everything they said by way of criticism of Pitt, especially as a war leader, strengthened suspicions that at heart they were sympathisers with the French, men who wished to see British armies and fleets defeated if the outcome of such disasters was a change of government. George III's assessment of Fox as an irresponsible opportunist was endorsed by the majority of the political nation. But although the Foxites failed in the practice of politics they succeeded in creating a myth. Like other frustrated politicians seeing the chance of office receding with every year that passed, they took refuge in wild assertions, repeating old accusations of the dangers posed by the influence of the crown, with Pitt cast in North's old role as the agent of corruption. While corruption was being sustained by repression, an assault upon traditional liberties was being masked by the unnecessary prolongation of a futile war. What was in essence a series of mistaken political gambles came to be elevated to the status of a noble crusade; the uncertain fumbling of opposition was presented as a brave struggle against an aggressive executive and a repressive regime dominated by reaction and motivated by fear. Historians with little awareness and no experience of ideological war, attracted by the suggestion that there ought to have been an alternative to the long war against France, bathed Fox's long years in opposition with the romantic haze of selfless devotion to the cause of peace. Fox was represented as virtually a pacifist, which was not the case, or as a Victorian liberal ahead of his time, which was as inaccurate as it was anachronistic. The truth was less noble and much more stark: Fox had taken another gamble, and once again he had lost.

In the closing years of the eighteenth century Pitt was preoccupied with two areas of policy: the war and the Irish problem. The two were inextricably connected, each complicating the other. Although it became clear that Britain could deny victory to the French, British control of the sea making it impossible for the French to mount any full-scale invasion of Britain, it was evident that Britain alone could not defeat France. Only in alliance with a major power or powers on the Continent would it be possible for Britain to defeat the French. When the French became entangled in Bonaparte's over-ambitious Egyptian campaign – an adventure forced upon the French by Britain's command of the sea and their own need to break out of the consequent deadlock – the British sought once again to build up a grand coalition against France. Grenville was fully committed to this strategy, possibly more so than any other minister. Dundas, the war secretary, was always more sceptical, uneasy about anything which had the flavour of impracticable boldness or grandiose phantasy. Pitt came to believe that a second coalition could and should be created and that its chances of success were good. British sea power and British gold would combine to persuade Austria and Russia to commit their armies to a sustained assault upon the French. At first all seemed to go well, but once Bonaparte returned from Egypt (even without his army) the French reversed the trend of campaigns in Europe. The battles of Hohenlinden and Marengo restored French fortunes in Germany and Italy. Austria was forced to make peace; Russia dropped out of the war. Although Nelson's victory at Copenhagen denied the Danish fleet to the French the familiar stalemate was restored, with France supreme on land and Britain unassailable at sea. The consequences for the British government were momentous. Pitt was downhearted at the failure to break the familiar deadlock; Grenville swung from excessive optimism to gloom and despondency; Dundas felt that events had justified his caution. Worst of all, it was clear that Pitt's health was failing. Even those who had no love for the Foxites began to suspect that Pitt had lost his touch, his capacity to command events, his subtle mastery of the craft of politics. The strategy represented by the second coalition was in tatters. Pitt was not ideologically opposed to peace with France, but previous experience had shown that the chances of a reasonable or lasting peace were negligible whenever negotiations were carried on in the aftermath of French victories, when French pride was rampant and the self-confidence of her rulers inflamed by success.

Ireland and Union

While the disappointments of war wore down Pitt's stamina and added to the grievous burdens which he had borne so bravely for so long, the

Irish problem added a complicating factor which was eventually to divide the ministry in such a way as to make Pitt's continuation in office impossible. Here Pitt paid the price, not of undue caution, but of attempting to carry a major reform in a situation of complexity and confusion. Even in the late 1780s Pitt had been conscious of the defects of the so-called constitutional settlement of 1782, which the Rockinghamites had flattered themselves as affording a solution to the Irish problem. Nothing was further from the truth. Legislative independence for the Dublin parliament threw various anomalies into greater relief. Pitt found the Irish parliament obstructive over his proposals for Irish free trade and defiant over his approach to the problems of the regency. While the Westminster parliament had accepted the Pittite case for a limited regency by authority of an act of parliament, the legislature at Dublin had followed the Foxite line. Had George III's illness lasted a little longer, the Irish would have invested the Prince as regent with unlimited powers as of right. The French Revolution had added further complications to the already complex Irish situation. The United Irishmen, impatient with the constitutionalist approach of Irish Whigs such as Henry Grattan, saw in the ideas of 1789 the key to the unravelling of the Irish problem. A non-sectarian republic on the French model would unite the communities in Ireland. French help would procure the severance of the link with Britain. Republicanism and separatism replaced legislative independence and partnership as the objectives which appealed to many young Irish patriots.

Pitt sought to meet the challenge by pushing through civil rights legislation in Dublin and by enfranchising the Catholic freeholders of Ireland. These initiatives were not popular in the Irish parliament, where the reforms insisted upon by the British government were widely resented. The fiasco of Earl Fitzwilliam's lord lieutenancy heightened the attraction of the United Irishmen to those disillusioned with the prospects for constitutional change. In 1795 Fitzwilliam provoked a major crisis in Dublin by mishandling the question of Catholic relief. He was a convinced advocate of Catholic emancipation – the admission of Catholics to public office and to parliament – and he had been sent to Ireland to prepare the ground for a measure of relief. But he succeeded only in antagonising Protestants and disappointing Catholics. By dismissing known opponents of Catholic emancipation he raised Catholic hopes without being able to fulfil them. Amid stormy controversy he resigned as lord lieutenant. By his errors of judgement Fitzwilliam made it more difficult for any British government to carry into effect the policy which he had so zealously favoured. The United Irishmen exploited the situation to the full. It seemed that the Catholic majority in Ireland had nothing to hope for from the British government. Plans for a rising in collusion with the French were drawn up. But the authorities anticipated the rebels' schemes. In Ulster General Lake disarmed the peasantry with brutal effectiveness. Several of the leaders of the United Irishmen were arrested; others fled to France. The most prominent and engaging of the Irish patriots, Lord Edward Fitzgerald, died of wounds received while resisting arrest. When the rebellion came in 1798, its most serious manifestation was confined to a single province, the outbreaks of republican frenzy being quickly contained elsewhere. The hoped-for help from France did not arrive until it was too late, and even then in insufficient strength. The rising was crushed, but at a bloody cost. What the United Irishmen had envisaged as a great national rising had reverted to a savage series of rural disorders, intercommunal hatred expressing itself in mutual atrocity.

The credibility of the Dublin parliament was further eroded. Protestants who had little love for the dominance of the British had been compelled to ask the British government for help. The legacy of the rebellion was one of intensified bitterness. Pitt believed that the rebellion had so transformed the Irish situation that there was no hope of restoring the status quo. He turned to a parliamentary union as the solution to the problem, modelling his proposals on the successful Union with Scotland. Pitt and his colleagues saw Union as part of a comprehensive policy. It was not intended to stand alone. But Pitt knew how disastrous it would be formally to incorporate proposals for Catholic emancipation into the Union Bill. He hoped that, once the Union was accomplished, commercial and economic concessions and a new initiative to tackle religious disaffection would lead directly to benefits which would improve the lot of the people and ease community relations.

At Westminster the Union went through without trouble, but in Dublin the Bill was carried only after a prolonged struggle. Only at the second attempt was a majority sufficient for the Union achieved in the Irish House of Commons. During the campaign to carry the Bill, Cornwallis, the lord lieutenant, and Castlereagh, the Irish secretary, had refrained from giving formal promises to the Catholics that the Union would inevitably mean emancipation. But they had implied that the chances of relief would be greater once the Union came into effect, the imperial legislature being better equipped to take a broad view of the issue than the Dublin parliament had been. Compensation had also been paid to those Irish boroughmongers and patrons who would lose their parliamentary seats as a result of the Union. This was an indication of the sensitivity over charter and property rights which was so marked a feature of the period. In one sense the Irish Union amounted to a substantial measure of parliamentary reform. One of the most forbidding barriers to any pattern of disfranchisement was the contemporary belief that it was unjust to deprive men of their charter or property rights without compensation. Even those who resisted the Irish Union to the bitter end were eager to accept the proffered compensation. It is inaccurate to suggest that only the distribution of patronage on a vast scale ensured the passage of the measure. It is nearer the truth to recognise that contemporary values made it impossible to reduce the number of parliamentary constituencies without regard for the rights of those who were being deprived of the privilege of returning MPs to parliament. But even when he had successfully accomplished the parliamentary union, Pitt had to face considerable opposition to the measure which he believed to be a necessary sequence to the Union with Ireland: the admission of Catholics to the imperial parliament.

Catholic Emancipation and the Fall of Pitt

Pitt knew that George III disapproved of Catholic emancipation. The King made no secret of his conviction that his coronation oath committed him to upholding the established churches in each of his dominions, and he was convinced that to admit Catholics to public office would infringe his undertaking to defend the privileges of the Protestant reformed religion established by law. Pitt therefore came to the conclusion that his chances of success would be greater if he approached the King only after he had obtained the support of the cabinet. This meant raising the issue in cabinet before putting it to the King. Pitt knew that this involved an element of risk, but during the war he had often discussed matters in cabinet without raising them with the King first. This did not imply any wish on Pitt's part formally to confine or limit the role of the crown. It was rather a reflection of the pressures imposed upon him by circumstances. Pitt was not seeking to apply any coordinated constitutional theory. He thought that the Catholic question could be tackled in much the same way as any other, and in choosing the method of handling it his chief object was to make success more likely.

But Pitt ran into massive difficulties. Opinion within the cabinet was divided. If the King's objections could be overcome, it was possible that the ministers would agree to allow the issue to go forward, but Pitt seriously underestimated the hostility with which Loughborough, the lord chancellor, opposed the granting of Catholic relief. Loughborough believed that Catholic emancipation would be a major breach in the constitutional settlement established in the aftermath of the Glorious Revolution. It would make a fundamental innovation in constitutional law and practice, and one innovation could well lead to others. As the King's legal and constitutional adviser he was fully cognisant of George III's convictions. While the King was on holiday at Weymouth, Loughborough took the opportunity of alerting him as to what was being discussed in the cabinet. The King was angry. He was shocked that such a major change was being discussed by his ministers without prior consultation. Loughborough succeeded in inflaming the King's prejudices, and in convincing him that fidelity to his coronation oath rendered any possibility of agreeing to Catholic emancipation wholly out of the question. It was soon public knowledge that George III was outraged by what his ministers had been contemplating. The King's intervention was decisive. Those who were lukewarm over the proposed measure had no desire to challenge the King, while those who were hostile to it welcomed his affirmations of loyalty to the Protestant establishment in church and state. At a public levée, George III's comments about Castlereagh and Catholic relief were emotional and violently hostile.

Pitt found that instead of being able to approach the King with the support of his colleagues, he now faced a revolt against his proposals in the cabinet. There was disturbing evidence that in the country at large opposition was vocal and gathering strength and momentum. Once again George III had voiced the anxieties of the political nation. Yet Pitt felt that he could not quietly drop emancipation. Although he had not given any formal promise to the Catholic community, either in Britain or Ireland, he felt morally bound on the issue. Nor did he feel that he could defer the matter and carry on as first minister. He knew that he had lost the confidence of the King, the foundation on which his political career and his achievements as a minister had been grounded. It is possible that Pitt's will to continue in office was now broken, albeit temporarily. His health was poor. Although it is difficult to be dogmatic, any diagnosis being highly speculative, it is possible that he was already suffering from the cancer which killed him in 1806. Even if this were not the case, Pitt was suffering from mental and physical exhaustion. He had seen his hopes of victory in the war dashed. Now the outcome of the controversy over Catholic relief cast doubts on his political judgement and his ability to ascertain the mood of his colleagues and carry them with him – an aptitude which had earlier contributed greatly to his political success. Historians have sometimes suggested that Pitt ought to have handled the question of Catholic relief in some other way. But there was little likelihood that any alternative available to him would have led to a happier conclusion. Incorporating Catholic emancipation in the Irish Act of Union would almost certainly have ensured the failure of that measure in the Dublin parliament; possibly in the Westminster parliament too. Pitt had underestimated the depth and range of hostility to Catholic relief. He had mistaken the extent to which George III represented majority opinion within the political nation and almost certainly the nation at large. He had also miscalculated what the impact of public opposition by the King would be on opinion within the cabinet.

It has sometimes been suggested that Pitt exploited the Catholic issue in order to extricate himself from office and thus free himself from the dire necessity of negotiating a peace with the hated French. Such a machiavellian interpretation of Pitt's motives is unconvincing. He had never been opposed in principle to a negotiated peace. He had attempted to negotiate a peace on previous occasions and, despite his disappointments, he was in no sense precluded from doing so again. He later fully supported Addington in the negotiations which led to the Peace of Amiens. It may be nearer the mark to say that Pitt was exhausted, that defeat over the Catholic issue destroyed his habitual relish for the stratagems and struggles of public life. Once he saw that he had lost the confidence of the King it was understandable for him to feel that he could not carry on. Over many years he had been sustained by the trust of the King; now he was destroyed by George III's ostentatious withdrawal of his support. He knew that without the backing of his colleagues he could not challenge the King on an issue which had so many political and constitutional implications. In going out of office Pitt was recognising that his long tenure of power had been based on his capacity to make the traditional system work. Now that he no longer possessed the assured endorsement of George III, he could not command the loyalty of his ministerial colleagues. He had little choice but to accept the inevitable and resign. By temperament he was not a man to make futile gestures. A realist to the end, and respectful of the prerogatives of the crown, he accepted defeat because there was no chance of carrying on in office with any hope of restoring his own fortunes or the standing of his government. He had always defended the place of the crown in government. He had never affirmed a doctrine of prime ministerial dominance or a tightening of collective responsibility. He had never insisted that cabinets should be appointed or dismissed collectively. Most decisively of all, he had never sought to build up his party in the Commons. About 50 MPs looked to him as their leader, but not all of these would do so if he ceased to be first minister. His appeal had been to the court interest and the independents. Without the support of the King he was ill-equipped to appeal to either. He was compelled to admit that the mood of the House of Commons, and the mood of the country, were hostile to Catholic relief. In deferring to the King's verdict Pitt sadly admitted that he was submitting to the judgement of the nation.

Interpreting Pitt's conduct has been made more difficult because of the promise which he subsequently gave to George III that he would never raise the Catholic question again during the King's lifetime. This has sometimes been seen as further evidence of Pitt's selfishness and cunning, proof of the insincerity of his advocacy of the Catholic cause. This is to ignore the skill and ruthlessness with which George III exploited the deferential feelings and the exhausted state of his former minister. In 1801 George III had another bout of illness. On recovering, he told Pitt that it had been Pitt's insistence on bringing forward Catholic emancipation which had caused his own breakdown. Pitt had a regard for the King which the crisis had not diminished. He was deeply troubled by the possibility that anything he had done had shattered the King's health. He felt compelling reasons, therefore, to humour the King. As a politician he was also willing to look facts in the face. After what had happened, Pitt knew that as long as George III reigned there was absolutely no possibility of carrying Catholic emancipation. But the King was now elderly and his health was failing. It seemed to be doing little more than recognising the incontrovertible to give the King the promise for which he asked. Similar undertakings were given, at various times and either absolutely or implicitly, by Castlereagh, Canning and Tierney. Fox and Grenville refused, but it is worth noting that when the Talents took office on Pitt's death in 1806 Fox warned his colleagues of the dangers of bringing forward the Catholic question prematurely. Even politicians who had no wish to compromise themselves by acceding to the King's wishes knew that George III constituted an immovable obstacle to Catholic relief. Pitt knew that if he refused to give the requested promise, which meant much to the King, it would be much less likely that George III would turn to him as a possible first minister on a future occasion. He also knew that to deny the King such a reassurance would be seen as heartless indifference to the feelings of a sick and ageing monarch. Pitt was not seeking an early return to office. Throughout the Addington ministry he was content to be a backbencher. By giving his promise to George III he was merely recognising the realities of the political situation. No one anticipated that George III would outlive Pitt – and Fox, too, for that matter.

What is true is that George III parted with his chief minister with a remarkable lack of regret, considering the seventeen years during which Pitt had served the crown and the circumstances in which George III had called Pitt to the premiership in the first place. Possibly this was a sign that the King regarded the Catholic question as so fundamental that it transcended personal feelings and any lesser loyalties. But the King could not have parted with Pitt as he did had he not had an acceptable alternative minister available in the person of Henry Addington. The willingness of several of Pitt's colleagues to serve under Addington strengthened the King's hand still further. Although Grenville, Dundas, Castlereagh, Canning and Cornwallis all resigned their various offices, Pitt's failure to carry the cabinet with him reflected the traditionalism which was still dominant in attitudes towards the conventions of the constitution. At the beginning of Pitt's premiership his colleagues had not felt that they owed their appointment to him: they had seen themselves as sharing with him the responsibility of responding to the demands which the King was making of them. The same was true for many members of Pitt's government in 1801. They had been willing to serve under Pitt. They shared his stance on the war, the role of the crown in government, the dubious nature of party and formed opposition. But they reserved the right to follow their own inclinations on matters of policy outside the fiscal, military or diplomatic responsibilities of government. For men such as Chatham, Westmorland, Portland and Liverpool the Catholic question raised questions of a conscientious nature. Had it been possible to carry emancipation without public controversy, acquiescence in such a policy might have been possible, but it seemed better to part company with Pitt rather than allowing the Catholic question to become central in a long and protracted debate. Portland, Eldon, and Loughborough sincerely rejected Catholic relief, just as they rejected repealing the Test and Corporation Acts, because such initiatives represented inroads into the Revolution Settlement. Catholic emancipation had been brought forward in the context of Irish policy; it was legitimate to doubt whether the granting of relief would necessarily have had all the beneficial consequences in Ireland which its supporters claimed that it would.

Only a handful of his colleagues ever came near to penetrating Pitt's aloofness and reserve. Dundas and Grenville had been the closest to him, but those who were not within the charmed circle resented the dominance of one man. It is significant that Pitt's most loyal supporters were either closely associated with him in the highest reaches of government, or were young men of promise, such as Castlereagh and Canning. Despite his reserve, Pitt always had a keen eye for politicians of ability. He had no hesitations about bringing such men forward, despite their relative youth. But his relationships with those in the middle ranks of government were less sure. This was compounded by his neglect to build up a party in the Commons, a failure which was criticised by Canning during the Addington administration. In general, Pitt's assumptions about the conduct of politics were as conventional as they had been twenty years before, when he had entered politics.

But there was one area in which reflection upon what had happened to him brought Pitt to contemplate a degree of innovation. This concerned the relationship of the prime minister to the cabinet. In 1803, in conversations with Dundas, who had been raised to the peerage as Lord Melville, Pitt confessed that it was expedient that the chief weight in council and the principal place in the confidence of the King should rest with a first minister who should also be at the head of the finances. If a clash of opinion should take place within the cabinet the sentiments of the minister should prevail, the dissentient members of the government being free to act as their consciences directed in such circumstances. For many years these comments of Pitt were usually interpreted as a description of how he had conducted his government during his first administration. It is more convincing to see in these remarks a response to what had happened during the crisis over Catholic emancipation. Pitt was attempting to formulate a set of conventions which would prevent a recurrence of the events which had forced him to resign. He had come to realise that the primacy of the first minister had to be more formally and more generally recognised. He still failed to spell out all the implications of his proposal, particularly as it affected the appointment and dismissal of ministers, and nothing he said to Melville compromised the King's legitimate freedom of choice in the selection of a prime minister. That initiative would still lie with the King. Nor did Pitt imply that the leadership of any party was to be associated with the type of primacy he had in mind. It was very much the reluctant concession of a conservative but practically-minded politician of long experience and exceptional gifts to the necessity of making modest changes in constitutional practice in order to make the functioning of government smoother, less vulnerable to internal dissension, and less open to intrigue.

Pitt's resignation had been a victory for George III in a constitutional as well as a political sense. It showed that the King retained the inalienable right, which George III believed he had inherited under the Revolution Settlement, and which was vested in the crown for all time, to choose and dismiss his ministers and to veto, either formally or informally, legislation put forward by his servants. Only the Foxites talked of checking or limiting these powers. Even when they suffered embarrassment or frustration the majority of mainstream politicians clung to the belief that the legitimate prerogatives of the crown were essential to the effective working of the institutions and organs of government. Although the King was no longer involved in day-to-day matters of routine, he was still expected to be the prime mover in the search for and in the establishment of any administration, and his confidence was seen as essential for the survival and functioning of any government. These assumptions were a natural expression of that preoccupation with administration rather than legislation which was the first concern of all politicians. Just as the pressures of government during a long and exhausting war had led Pitt to govern increasingly through a small inner group within the cabinet and with less formal regard for the regular involvement of the King, so the desire to see the King's government carried on with as little disruption as possible dominated the outlook of most practising politicians, who had their sights firmly set on the attainment of office. Their motives for seeking office were mixed. For some the service of the crown was primary; for others the achievement of status, the enjoyment of patronage and power, the recognition of what they felt was their rightful place in the political nation. For virtually none of them, the Foxites included, was a political career the means by which some visionary dream or utopian ideal was to be realised. For most politicians the motives and expectations which impelled them to indulge in political activity were a blend of conscious aspirations with those less-rational assumptions which they had inherited from the manner in which politics had been practised for something like a century.

Dramatic though many of the events between the fall of North and the resignation of Pitt had been, the structure of politics still retained a familiar character. The prerogatives and influence of the crown remained important, and at times decisive. There was considerable ambiguity about the extent to which members of the cabinet owed a primary loyalty to the first minister of the day. Cabinets were not normally appointed or dismissed collectively. The replacement of Pitt by Addington represented a major reshuffle rather than a total change. Collective responsibility on policy was limited to the traditional areas of finance, foreign policy and defence. On other matters – the slave trade, parliamentary reform, religious disabilities – ministers claimed and resolutely exercised what they believed was a legitimate freedom to go their own way, without this putting in doubt their continued membership of the administration. The party system, if that is the right term, which is questionable, was a matter of several groupings, not two major parties. The Foxites, who were a tiny band of about 60 in 1801, prided themselves on their consistency, their loyalty to the Whig tradition, and their devotion to curbing the influence of the crown, but they were more remote than ever from any hope of achieving office. Pitt's fall had not advanced their prospects. George III's hostility towards them was greater than ever. Like many of his subjects the King regarded the Foxites as defeatist over the war, irresponsible in their conduct of opposition, and unreliable on almost every matter of public concern. The Foxites were not of one mind on parliamentary reform, and although most of them supported Catholic relief, they did so with varying degrees of enthusiasm and for a variety of reasons. They were incapable of practising their own doctrines of opposition, having been compelled to rely on tactics as backward-looking as the reversionary interest and a parliamentary secession. Nor can politics be seen in terms of a Foxite-versus-Pittite alignment. Important though the Pittites were, they were only one of several parliamentary groups. Pitt was accepted as leader by a small group of MPs, some of whom resented his failure to build up his personal following, while others were content to look to him for leadership precisely because his views were traditional ones. To the end of his life Pitt retained a disdain for party inherited from his father. This endeared him to some, giving him the status of a national statesman rather than a party politician. Many MPs distrusted Pitt as too arrogant and self-possessed a figure. They preferred government to be in the hands of someone like Addington, whose assumptions were acceptable to backbench country gentlemen, and whose conduct was less likely to lead to controversy, embittered debate, or a challenge to vested interests.

During the Addington administration Grenville came to act more and more independently of Pitt. Soon it was possible to speak once again of a distinct Grenvillite group. Grenville, like Pitt, had been identified with the defence of the country's institutions against the French, and once the war had started he was committed to working for the defeat of the

French. Like his cousin, Grenville was committed to Catholic relief, and he was even more insistent than Pitt that nothing should be said or done which would compromise his stance. Addington's strength as first minister lay in the confidence of the King, not in any party following. He had his own group, but it was small in numbers. Like Pitt before him, Addington was dependent on the support of the court interest and on appealing to independents. As for the conservative Whigs their fortunes had been startlingly mixed during the war years. Portland had remained loyal to Pitt, once he had taken the drastic step of agreeing to work with him. As home secretary he had been prominent in beating off the challenge of Jacobinism. But he was not in any true sense a Pittite. He was content to serve as home secretary under Addington before moving to be lord president of the council. He was opposed both to parliamentary reform and to Catholic emancipation, just as he had been when he had acted in concert with Fox. Fitzwilliam, on the other hand, after the bitter experience of his Irish lord lieutenancy, was moving back to an understanding with Fox. Once peace came, reconciliation between the two old friends was much easier. The Catholic issue was one on which Fox and Fitzwilliam were of one mind. At the same time, despite their debt to Pitt, the younger Pittites did not feel under any obligation to stay out of office indefinitely. Committed though he was to Catholic relief, and to other reforms in Ireland such as the commutation of tithes and the payment of Catholic clergy by the state, Castlereagh, for example, felt free to accept office in October 1802 as president of the board of control under Addington. It is hard to see any two-party system, however nascent, manifesting itself in such diverse permutations. Pitt did not expect his younger followers to deny themselves office. Appreciating their talents as he did he was generous enough to encourage them to serve the crown in their own fashion. Besides, whatever experience they gained in office would be of value in the years that lay ahead.

Politics were dominated by a need to find a government which was able, in general terms, to appeal to a broad range of support. Similarly, there were those who, faced by a particular administration, regarded themselves as being in opposition to it. But this did not constitute a two-party system, in the sense usually carried by that expression today; that is, the dominance of politics by two parties, one of which is in office, fully assured that party organisation and discipline will provide a working majority in the Commons in virtually all circumstances, while the other party seeks to turn out the government, each using techniques of

communication and electoral management to win a sufficient proportion of votes from a mass electorate to settle the issue at a general
election. In Pitt's day both government and opposition were shifting
coalitions of differing groups, united only on particular issues while
compelled to accept differences of opinion on others, and pledged only
loosely habitually to act with each other. To talk of ideological differences is unconvincing. The majority of politicians, whether they longed
for office or whether they were content to serve as backbenchers whose
chief anxiety was to safeguard local interests, were 'Whig' in their
presuppositions. Fidelity to the main features of the Revolution Settlement was taken for granted. It was in some ways absurd that first the
Rockinghamites and then the Foxites asserted the right to monopolise
the designation of Whig. Pittites, Foxites, Portlandites, Addingtonians,
Grenvillites and the mass of parliamentary independents all shared
conventional presuppositions about the balanced constitution, the nature
of representation, the indelible link between property and liberty, each
being a healthy security for the other. The real challenge to this formidable consensus came from the popular radicals, especially those who
affirmed Painite notions of natural right and who argued, not only that
parliament needed to be reformed but that the entire system should be
democratised.

The war gave the misleading impression that Pitt presided over a
massive personal following in the Commons. In most situations and on
most issues the overwhelming majority of the House supported Pitt and
were willing to give him their confidence as the most efficient and the
most effective minister available. But this did not mean that they
regarded themselves as members of Pitt's personal following. The Catholic controversy demonstrated that when Pitt questioned or defied the
prevalent consensus, and especially when he came into conflict with the
King by doing so, the majority of MPs placed their loyalty to the constitution, however unimaginatively defined or crudely understood, and
their duty to the King, which remained absolute, above any loyalty to the
minister of the day. The ageing and ailing George III still commanded
the affection of his subjects and the respect of members of the House of
Commons in a fashion which was prior to the loyalty which men were
prepared to give to any politician, however eminent and however
experienced. Those issues which later generations regarded as being the
most significant – the reform of parliament, the abolition of the slave trade,
relief for Catholics and Dissenters, even the conduct of the war itself –
did not neatly dovetail with those affections, affinities and alliances

which moulded political behaviour. Coalition persisted as a fact of political life, much more so than party, because no party could hope to form an effective government without establishing some sort of understanding with at least one, and usually more than one, of the other political groups. As long as George III remained active, performing his constitutional duty with all the devotion dictated by conviction and conscience, the mode of political conduct continued to conform to a pattern more reminiscent of the past than indicative of the future. As long as the majority of MPs, whatever their party, did not owe their election to party affiliation or to party organisation, they were able to exercise a welcome and cherished freedom in how they reacted to the constantly changing alignments among competing political rivals. The Commons were aware of opinion in the political nation, but they did not feel obliged absolutely to defer to it. Once elected, the House of Commons was for all practical purposes synonymous with the political nation. MPs were free to exercise their own judgement on events, personalities and controversies and to act accordingly. Nothing was more hateful to backbenchers than the demand that MPs should cease to be representatives and instead become delegates, answerable for their conduct to organised bodies of opinion outside the House. Nothing was more abhorrent than suggestions that a mass electorate should dictate to the House of Commons, which would then be reduced to being the mere agent of the popular voice. The independence of the House of Commons was still seen as the best security for the nation's liberties. A respect for independence, both personal and collective, made men wary of party. It was, of course, inevitable that in politics men should act in concert with others. A chaotic individualism was both undesirable and unworkable. But at the end of the eighteenth century the House of Commons was dominated not by two parties but by a multiplicity of parties, with only the small Foxite group arguing the case for formal opposition and the collective appointment of cabinets. However controversial some of his actions, and however regrettable some of his prejudices, George III was not fighting a lonely battle against an established party system. He was merely doing what he and the majority of MPs believed was his constitutional duty, which he was expected to perform in familiar and conventional ways. The first question asked about any potential prime minister was not whether his party had a majority in the House of Commons; the first preoccupation was whether candidates for the premiership had the confidence of the King. This was the primary requirement and the one consideration which more than any other decided whether a majority of MPs were willing to give an administration the opportunity of proving itself capable of government. It was, therefore, not surprising that there should be times when it was far from easy to find a ministry which could win the confidence of the King and the support of the Commons. The creation and survival of ministries continued to be difficult, fraught with accident, and vulnerable to the tides and eddies of fortune.

3

THE SEARCH FOR A MINISTRY

For a decade after the resignation of Pitt, the country was ruled by a succession of shortlived ministries, all of them exposed to the impact of war, and all of them torn by internal dissensions and confusion. In some respect these years were reminiscent of the first ten years of George III's reign, but because of the war, and perhaps because of the depressing experience of the 'Ministry of All the Talents', only the most embittered Foxites and Grenvillites blamed the King for the failure to find a minister capable of retaining the royal confidence and the trust of the House of Commons for any significant length of time. The recurrence of ministerial instability reflected the confusions and uncertainties of the party system. Although Lord Liverpool eventually reunited most of those who claimed, in one way or another, to belong to the Pittite tradition, he was able to accomplish this only over a number of years, and because he showed outstanding powers of tact, restraint, and discretion in appealing to a variety of political groups, all of which liked to look back to Pitt in some respects but whose respect for each other was often streaked with remembered wrongs or past differences.

The Addington Ministry

The Pittite tradition had begun to fracture even before Pitt's death. Pitt himself had neglected to organise his own followers, relying somewhat blandly on his own talents and the appeal of his great name. For most of Addington's ministry he gave general approval to Addington's policies; only towards the end did he throw his considerable authority and prestige into the scales against his successor. Nor should the sneers, however brilliant, of George Canning be taken as an accurate summary of Adding-ton's capacities. Addington showed considerable skill in managing the national finances. In his administration of the property or income tax – that unpopular wartime expedient – he proved to be more competent than Pitt himself had been. Addington lacked charisma, the dramatic talents which could impress opinion both inside and outside parliament, but at the beginning of his ministry he gained the respect and earned the confidence of the majority of MPs. He had the endorsement of George III; he had won much goodwill as speaker of the House of Commons; his efforts to end the war were widely welcomed. After the failure of the second coalition to shatter the military supremacy of France most politi-cians accepted the desirability of some sort of peace with the French republic. The Peace of Amiens, stigmatised by Sheridan as the peace everybody was glad of and nobody was proud of, was no more than a rough and ready acceptance of French dominance in Europe and Brit-ish control of the seas. The probability is that Bonaparte regarded it as no more than a useful breathing space; an armistice, not a peace settle-ment. But once the peace was signed, many British tourists, including Fox, took the opportunity to visit France, and everyone hoped that, despite the ambiguities of the peace terms, there would be no need to resume the war. The British had promised to withdraw their garrison from Malta; the French to evacuate their forces from Piedmont and Naples. Neither side trusted the other, but since it seemed obvious that nothing could break the stalemate which had been so marked and so recurrent a feature of the contest between Britain and France, most people hoped that Amiens agreement would last.

Had the peace proved permanent Addington's ministry would almost certainly have been regarded as reasonably competent. Addington was soundly conservative on the Catholic question, which made him accept-able to George III, and he was able to rely on the support of those members of Pitt's administration who had not been pledged to back Pitt's advocacy of Catholic emancipation. Even so, Addington knew that it was essential for him to broaden his range of political support if his government were to survive for the foreseeable future. He did not object to bringing several of Pitt's followers into the ministry. In 1802 he persuaded Castlereagh to accept the presidency of the board of control. Other Pittites, such as Canning, held aloof, seeking to activate Pitt into taking the initiative to stiffen opposition to Addington. The Foxites jeered at Addington as a mediocrity, but writhed in frustration: the Peace of Amiens had brought them no nearer office. Though they claimed that the peace proved that their pleas for a negotiated settlement had been justified, throughout the 1790s the political nation regarded them with suspicion, and they still laboured under the double handicap of being dismissed as defeatists and opportunists.

The most significant development during the Addington administration was the emancipation of Grenville from his former subordination to Pitt. Grenville refused to follow his cousin in giving a promise to the King never to revive the issue of Catholic relief. With the disappointment of his hopes during the second coalition, Grenville became more convinced that any resumption of war would impose an impossible economic burden upon Britain. Although Grenville sniped at Addington's fiscal policies and had little confidence in his ability to maintain the peace, he had no desire to bring down Addington only to replace him with Pitt. He was more and more attracted to the prospect of a broad-based government of national unity. He was now more assured of his own abilities, more doubtful about Pitt's integrity, and more unsure about Pitt's motives. Grenville became convinced that if Pitt were to return as chief minister he should do so only if he were willing to preside over the most comprehensive coalition administration: only such a ministry, Grenville believed, held out any prospect of future success, whether at home or abroad. Those who had rallied behind Pitt during the dark years of the war and the gloomy anxieties of the anti Jacobin scare were now divided in several ways. Some were serving with Addington; others, including some who had accepted office under Addington, still looked primarily to Pitt for guidance; others refused to compromise their loyalty to Pitt, but were disappointed by his reluctance to play a decisive and leading role in opposition politics; others, led by Grenville, began to detach themselves from Pitt and to play a more independent part in politics. Meanwhile the Foxites looked on, disapproving of Addington but still suspicious of Pitt, and bitterly resentful of their own continued exclusion from the political mainstream. Pitt continued to behave as a man who disliked party, and who believed that if he were to be recalled to office this would happen because he held himself apart from party conflict, sustaining his reputation as a man who could be invited to form a patriotic government on a non-party basis. It would be wholly inadequate to say that George III created this state of affairs. The King believed that his own conduct throughout the crisis over Catholic relief had been entirely proper: if there had been any political sharp-practice the King saw it as having been instigated by Pitt and the other advocates of Catholic emancipation.

But it soon became apparent that the dominant issue facing the government was the familiar problem of Britain's relations with France. Even those who wished desperately for peace recognised that Bonaparte was behaving in a manner which challenged the assumptions on which the peace had been signed. Bonaparte intervened in Switzerland, where he proclaimed himself mediator of the Swiss republic. He did not withdraw his troops from the Italian duchies. Most seriously of all, from the British point of view, he was still manifestly interested in Egypt and the Near East. The publication of Sebastiani's Egyptian report in the official French newspaper, *Le Moniteur*, inflamed British suspicions of Bonaparte. For his part, the First Consul resented criticisms of him which appeared in the British press. He could not believe that these were not inspired by the British government. He had failed to take to heart Fox's assurances, made during the latter's visit to Paris, that the British press was free and not subject to official censorship. Addington had no wish to resume the war. He and his colleagues knew from bitter experience how difficult it would be to sustain another armed conflict with France. They feared the drain on national resources, and they recognised how impossible it would be for Britain to win a war without effective allies on the continent. But they felt that they could not ignore what appeared to be a serious and growing threat to British interests, especially in the Mediterranean.

They refused to hand over Malta to the Knights of St John, fearing that if they did so the island would soon be occupied by the French. Malta was the key to the Mediterranean. If the French seized Malta they would be well-placed to resume military operations in Egypt. Bonaparte's grandiose dreams of a French empire in the Near East and of a renewed French challenge to British interests in India had already led to the Egyptian expedition of 1798. Though that had failed, there were good reasons for assuming that a resumption of such a scheme was one of the options Bonaparte was actively contemplating. Believing that he was violating the spirit of the Amiens settlement Britain failed to comply with the letter of the treaty. Mutual suspicion ripened into mutual abuse. Lord Whitworth, the British ambassador in Paris, was publicly humiliated by Bonaparte. The British knew that they could not afford to yield over Malta, even though they were in technical breach of the peace treaty. They were also aware if the war were resumed it would not be a war merely over Malta. What was at stake was the balance of power in Europe. Dominance of the continent was the ultimate objective in Bonaparte's mind. As long as he exploited every chance to enlarge his influence and extend his power in Europe the British could not see peace as a viable option. In May 1803 Whitworth left Paris and the war was renewed.

Bonaparte shocked British opinion by interning some ten thousand British holidaymakers, in France when the war broke out. He claimed that many of these unfortunates were spies. The British regarded such actions as proof of what they had known all along: that Bonaparte did not respect the conventions of civilised intercourse between nations. The war was a different type of conflict from that waged against the Jacobin republic. Whereas in the 1790s it had been possible for some of Pitt's opponents and some British radicals to claim that despite the excesses of the Jacobins the ideals of the French Revolution were nevertheless admirable, and that all that was needed for France to rediscover these ideals was a period of peace, which would allow the French to settle their domestic affairs free from foreign interference, it was now evident that Bonaparte had jettisoned the humanitarianism as well as the liberalism of 1789. To the British he seemed all too like a French Cromwell, a general whose military genius and political ruthlessness had enabled him to snatch supreme power at a time of anarchy and confusion. The struggle against Bonaparte was essentially and clearly a clash of interests. Though he liked to stand forth as the enemy of absolutist regimes, particularly where these were of a traditional character, he represented the extension of French power in Europe in a cruder and less idealistic fashion than the Jacobins had done. When in 1804 he declared himself emperor of the French, crowning himself in a spectacular ceremony at Notre Dame, the rejection of republican ideals and the cult of imperial power seemed complete.

Addington faced immense problems in waging the war. He knew that Britain lacked the resources directly and immediately to challenge the French in Europe. He therefore sought to stand on the defensive. Britain's naval power would deny victory to the French. Possibly another period of stalemate would bring Napoleon to his senses. After the failure of the second coalition, most British politicians were conscious of the defects rather than the opportunities of coalition diplomacy. Napoleon sought to seize the initiative by pushing on with preparations for the invasion of England. He built a huge fleet of transports to ferry over the 'Army of England', which lay in camp, awaiting its opportunity of a crossing, above Boulogne. Although during the peace Addington's policies of financial economy and military and naval disarmament had been popular, he was now accused of leaving the country in a feeble position to resist Napoleon. Many of his critics grossly exaggerated the effect of his economies. Some who had been vocal in calling for a speedy return to a peacetime establishment were eager to blame Addington for every sign of unpreparedness. In many respects Addington became a convenient scapegoat for errors of judgement which had been virtually universal among British politicians.

But there were immense difficulties in organising a united and effective opposition to Addington. Pitt had disapproved of Addington's economies; Fox had supported them. Grenville criticised Addington's measures, but continued stubbornly to advocate Catholic relief. He feared that Addington would prove incapable of fighting the war, but he saw little alternative other than standing on the defensive. Grenville believed that an overbold strategy would be economically disastrous for Britain; past disappointments had made him gloomy and morose in his expectations of continental allies. The pressing needs of home defence ensured enthusiastic support for the volunteer movement, about 150 000 men offering themselves for service. Addington thoroughly approved of the volunteers, but their efficiency was questionable, and there were protracted and confused debates over the best means of improving recruitment to the regular army and to the militia. In April 1804 Pitt, Fox and the Grenvillites all went into the same lobby during a debate on the Irish militia bill. Addington bowed to events. He had no wish to stay in office only as the result of some wearisome intrigue or humiliating political negotiation.

In some ways he had been unjustly treated. His income tax, reimposed on the renewal of the war, was a better scheme than Pitt's, and although he had run down the navy his reorganisation of the army has found favour with some historians. Much of the bitterness surrounding his fall turned on the clash of personalities. Grenville, for example, wished to turn out Addington in order to establish an all-party administration. His initial candidate to head such a ministry had been Pitt. But he came to despair of Pitt's reluctance to take the lead in building up the opposition to Addington. Pitt seemed too indulgent to the man who had succeeded him as first minister, too inclined to assume that if Addington fell, the chief place in any new ministry would be his as of right. Grenville's dislike of Addington pushed him towards cooperation with Fox. At least they shared a common devotion to the cause of Catholic relief. But on other issues there were crucial differences between them. Grenville, however dispiritedly, supported the war against France; Fox, despite the disillusionment of the Amiens settlement, still talked as if a negotiated peace were there simply for the asking. Grenville's disappointment with Pitt, and Fox's aversion to his old rival, drew Grenville and Fox together in cautious cooperation rather than harmonious unity. Another strange coalition was being slowly cobbled together. In these complex and often petty exchanges and manoeuvres the most salient feature was the weary desperation of men struggling to reach a measure of mutual understanding, rather than any decisive crisis in the evolution of the two-party system.

Pitt Returns

Once Addington resigned, George III asked Pitt to form a new administration. This was inevitable, given the fact that the country was at war and that there was no possibility of Pitt reviving the Catholic controversy. Even in 1801 George III had hoped that Pitt would stay on – though only on the King's terms. Now Pitt wanted to establish a patriotic ministry on the broadest possible base. There was nothing unusual about this. One of the most familiar of political clichés was the assertion that the best government would be that which included all men of ability regardless of the political grouping to which they belonged. Grenville, likewise, approved such a government in principle, and under the pressures of war the desire for an all-party administration was virtually unanimous. Pitt hoped that Fox would be foreign secretary and Grenville the lord president of the council. Charles Grey was to be war secretary and the former Portland Whig, Spencer, first lord of the admiralty. Portland himself was listed as lord privy seal, while Fitzwilliam would be a secretary of state. Eldon was to be offered the lord chancellorship, while of Pitt's younger disciples Castlereagh was put forward as president of the board of control and Canning as Irish secretary. But the scheme foundered on the opposition of George III. The King vehemently objected to the appointment of Fox as foreign secretary. He retained his detestation of Fox. During the long struggle with France the King had seen Fox as irresponsible and defeatist. George III could not forget that Fox had once toasted the sovereignty of the people, in a political gesture which had been as futile as it was ill-advised.

Given the attitude of Fox towards Addington and towards the resumption of the war, the King's misgivings were understandable. Pitt respected the opinions and prejudices of the King, however much he might rue their consequences. Although he now wished the pre-eminence of the prime minister to be more formally recognised, he had no wish to infringe upon the King's legitimate choice in the appointment of ministers. Fox, who was now in some respects weary of politics, urged his friends to take office without him. They refused: loyalty to Fox was one of the few constant lights by which the Foxites could steer. Emotionally they could not bring themselves to go into office with Pitt, while leaving Fox outside. They knew that if they did so, and if the war were prolonged and the ministry protracted, it would mean the end of the Foxite party. After so many years they could not prefer office, however tempting to men who had known the futilities of opposition for so long, to the preservation of that party which they had so often claimed was the nation's security against the assertion of royal influence and the extension of the power of the executive.

Despite his own desire for an all-party administration, Grenville could not bring himself to take office without Fox. However strange their alliance, he felt bound to honour it. Perhaps he feared that Pitt would once again reassert his old dominance over him, if he were to serve in the ministry without Fox's reassuring presence. Grenville found that he had what he had once wanted – a ministry headed by Pitt – but it was now unacceptable to him because without Fox and the Foxites he could not regard it as the great national coalition which was necessary, in his view, for the successful conduct of the war. Yet over the war Grenville did not really agree with Fox. Grenville wanted an all-party ministry in order to ensure that the war was competently conducted, that it was supported by every major political grouping, and that it was directed by all the wisdom and expertise available. But faced with the choice between joining a ministry headed by Pitt, which was less than a fully comprehensive administration, and going into opposition with Fox, Grenville finally chose the latter course. Apart from hostility to Addington, suspicion of Pitt and loyalty to the cause of Catholic relief, there was little to bind Fox and Grenville together. Fox still hoped for peace. Once he was free from any likelihood of the restraints of office, he talked again of the need to explore every possibility for peace. Grenville wanted the war to be directed efficiently, though he had set ideas about what this meant, and he had few illusions about the ease or the speed with which any peace could be negotiated. His experience as foreign secretary made him distrustful of the shallow optimism which marred Fox's pronouncements on the chances for peace, and he never shared Fox's facile trust in Napoleon's good intentions. The two men disagreed on parliamentary reform, although this was not a pressing matter in

1804, and the Foxites themselves had never been of one mind on the issue. Grenville and Fox were both interested in economical reform, but Grenville was always eager to acquire new forms of patronage and did not like the thought of giving up useful sinecures for the sake of abstract principle. The coalition between Fox and Grenville was in some ways more improbable than the more notorious coalition between Fox and North. Yet it would be false to see the Grenvillites simply as a conservative drag on an otherwise liberal opposition. To do so would be to imply a wholly false alignment of the various political affinities within the political nation.

Far from being either conservative or liberal, reactionary or reformist, the main groups were dominated by the exigencies of war and finance, by the constraints imposed by the attitudes of the King, by a range of inherited loyalties and antipathies, and by the inevitable necessity, created by the parliamentary system, of having to act in a variety of alliances, however loose or however temporary, if there were to be any chance of attaining office and thus influencing events. No single group had anything like the strength required to maintain itself in office unaided. Although the combined Grenvillite and Foxite parties numbered about 150 in the House of Commons, this left them far short of the aggregate needed to seize office on their own account. Even among the Foxites there were various complications of attachment and sentiment. Those MPs gathered round Moira and Sheridan were, in some respects, rather like the party of the Prince of Wales. They had often acted with Fox in the past; now, recognising the importance of the Prince as George III grew older, and the continuing significance of the influence of the crown, they preferred to cultivate the heir to the throne without feeling compelled to defer to Fox's judgement on all occasions. Old quarrels and remembered slights intensified this tendency towards fragmentation.

Pitt was bitterly disappointed by Grenville's intransigent refusal to accept office. He bravely committed himself to carrying on, even if the effort were to cost him his life, but he knew how weak his administration was without the Foxites and Grenvillites. In January 1805 Addington returned to office as lord president. This was a measure of Pitt's vulnerability and of Addington's utility. But relations between Pitt and Addington were soured by the impeachment of Melville – Pitt's old friend Dundas – the politician who had been closer to Pitt for far longer than anyone else. Addington and his followers were determined to refute suggestions that everything wrong with the navy had been inherited from St Vincent's tenure of the admiralty during the Addington administration. Addington claimed that investigations raised doubts about Melville's probity while he had been treasurer of the navy. Melville had been guilty of negligence, but his political opponents and all who were eager to embarrass Pitt found it expedient to press the more serious charge of malversation of funds. Fox and Grenville were keen to exploit the government's weaknesses, partly because the Melville affair heightened tension between Pitt's supporters and those of Addington. By supporting demands for impeachment, the Fox–Grenville opposition could demonstrate its own apparent unity and reveal the divisions within the ministry. They would also be able to reclaim some standing as the advocates of retrenchment and honest government. Only the casting vote of the speaker allowed the impeachment to proceed, but Pitt had been humiliated. In one of the rare instances on which he lost control of his feelings in public, tears ran down Pitt's cheeks at the destruction of his old and loyal colleague. Although Melville was finally cleared, his political career was ruined. His successor at the Admiralty, Barham, proved to be an outstanding appointment, but his selection did not please the Addingtonians and, because of lingering resentment and disaffection, Addington resigned in the summer of 1805.

Pitt's ministry seemed all the more frail and fallible. Fox and Grenville even tried to exploit the Catholic question in order to intensify their attack on Pitt. By introducing a motion in favour of considering Catholic relief, they forced Pitt to say that, while he was not opposed in principle, the time was not ripe. Pitt was forced into an uneasy stance, but many backbenchers were disturbed by any revival of Catholic claims. The King's respect for the opposition was not enhanced by such conduct. George III rightly regarded them as willing to try anything in order to divide Pitt's ministry. Like most of his subjects, the King thought that politicians should be concentrating their efforts on winning the war rather than scoring dubious points off their political adversaries. The Foxites and Grenvillites seemed preoccupied with embarrassing Pitt rather than accomplishing anything more admirable. By 1805 the loyalist groups which had rallied round the patriotic cause in the 1790s had split into several factions, each jealous of the other: the Pittites, the Addingtonians, the Grenvillites, as well as other smaller groups, such as the Canningites, who were in some respects more Pittite than Pitt. When Pitt sought to broaden his ministry after the defection of Addington, George III remained staunchly opposed to any suggestion that Fox should join the government, even if this were the only price which would ensure Grenville's participation. The King's impatience with the politicians was understandable, but he failed to see the toll which government was taking of Pitt. The prime minister's health was failing; the burden which he had borne so nobly for so long was killing him. The only hope was for some decisive resolution of the war.

Pitt had taken the initiative by building up another coalition against France. He had learned something from the frustrations of the 1790s. In approaching Austria and Russia for aid, he sought to exploit British sea power in the Mediterranean. He did not wish the British war effort to be weakened by sideshows. He hoped to find a decisive weakness in the enemy's dispositions and to turn it to account. But it was far from easy to know where best to strike or where to commit Britain's small army. Once Pitt had succeeded in creating the third coalition Napoleon struck against it with all his customary dash and brilliance. All Pitt's hopes were ruined. Mack was forced to surrender at Ulm, and in December 1805 Napoleon defeated the combined Austrian and Russian armies at Austerlitz. Although Nelson's victory at Trafalgar had reinforced British supremacy at sea, and although the immediate threat of an invasion of Britain was dispersed, the third coalition fared no better than its predecessors. Austria was forced to make peace. Prussia, entering the war with maladroit timing, was crushed. After two bloody battles at Eylau and Friedland the French emperor and the Russian tsar came to terms. At their meeting at Tilsit they divided Europe into two spheres of influence. The Napoleonic empire was at the apogee of its might and glory.

The Ministry of All the Talents

By the time Tilsit underlined Napoleon's dominance on the Continent, both Pitt and Fox were dead. It is probable that Pitt was suffering from cancer. In January 1806 he died, worn out by his exertions and disappointed of all his hopes. George III knew that he had no alternative but to send for Grenville, and that this inevitably meant accepting Fox as foreign secretary. When Fox and the King met, both put on as good a face as possible. They had little choice but to let bygones be bygones. Ironically George III soon found working with Fox congenial and acceptable, and when Fox died the King confessed that he had not thought he would miss him so much. Those who had been close to Pitt knew that Grenville's appointment meant their own return to the backbenches, but Grenville's ministry included Sidmouth (as Addington had now become) as lord privy seal and Spencer as home secretary. Of the younger men Lord Henry Petty became chancellor of the exchequer and Charles Grey first lord of the admiralty. To such a ministry 'the Ministry of All the Talents' was a misnomer, for several men of ability – Canning, Castlereagh, Hawkesbury – were outside it, but it was much more than a government composed of Foxites and Grenvillites. It represented Grenville's belief that the war called for as broadly-based a ministry as was possible, given the realities of politics. This comprehensiveness actually led to conflicts of opinion within the government. Old rivalries could not be forgotten overnight and there were clashes of personality and differences of temperament to compound ancient political quarrels.

The ministry proved to be a singularly unfortunate one. Almost everything it attempted ended in frustration and disappointment. Fox still yearned for peace. Grenville, who was much more experienced in dealing with the French, was sceptical of the chances of a successful negotiation, but in the aftermath of Napoleon's great victories he was even more pessimistic about the continuation of the war. Throughout the abortive negotiations Napoleon seized the initiative and never lost it. His motives were tactical. He wanted to isolate Britain from the powers of the Continent, particularly Russia. Talleyrand conducted the negotiations with his customary blend of subtlety and unscrupulousness. Yarmouth, who owed his place as one of the British negotiators to the fact that he had been interned as a British tourist stranded in France on the resumption of hostilities, was constantly duped by Talleyrand. Lauderdale – a close friend of Fox, of whom Sheridan once said that a joke in Lauderdale's mouth was no laughing matter – was also incapable of matching Talleyrand in the intricacies of diplomacy. The situation was made worse by Fox's serious illness. The truth was that he was dying. It may have been that, like Pitt, he had cancer. Although in the last weeks of his life Fox had the satisfaction of knowing that the House of Commons had voted in favour of abolishing the slave trade, his hopes for peace were wrecked. Fox's death in September 1806 led to Grey – now known by his courtesy title of Lord Howick – succeeding his old friend as foreign secretary. The Talents found it no easier than Pitt to wage war against Napoleon. French dominance in Europe was virtually complete. Expeditions to South America and to Egypt ended in disaster. The ministers knew neither how to end the war, since the peace talks ended in acrimony and failure, nor how to win it.

The ministry fell, not because of the stalemate which had once again descended upon the conduct of hostilities, but because of their own ill judged and badly-handled attempt to carry a limited measure of Catholic relief. They had hoped to carry legislation permitting Catholics to serve in senior commissioned ranks in the army. In itself this was a sensible proposal, but it was bungled. The ministers seemed unsure about the exact meaning of what it was they were proposing. Faced with criticism in the Commons they shuffled uneasily in order to fudge the issue. Worst of all they antagonised the King. George III became convinced that what was afoot was a shady conspiracy to carry a measure of Catholic relief without keeping him fully briefed. George III had good grounds for his anxiety, not because the ministers were being machiavellian, but because they were confused and uncertain. At first it had appeared that Catholics would not be promoted to staff rank; then the government contemplated opening up appointments to rank of general to Catholics and to extend the privilege to the navy by making Catholics eligible for promotion to the rank of admiral. Sidmouth was deeply unhappy about the situation. He thought that the pro-Catholics in the ministry were acting deviously, and he helped to stiffen the King's opposition. Addington feared that his colleagues were exploiting the Catholic question in the hope of tempting pro-Catholic Pittites, such as Canning, into joining them. Portland told the King to resist what Grenville was proposing. Had Fox been alive he might have prevented such a sorry sequence of errors and misjudgements. He had never given a formal promise never to raise the Catholic question again during the lifetime of George III, but when the Talents had taken office he had urged his friends not to bring forward the Catholic issue prematurely. He had been aware of the pitfalls facing the new administration, and especially sensitive about the potential dangers posed by the Catholic problem. Fox's principles were always more flexible in practice than in theory. He had compromised his reputation as a reformer by pleading with the House of Commons to permit Grenville to retain sinecure posts while being appointed first lord of the treasury. He knew that no principle could be absolutely unchangeable; once politicians were in office they would be compelled to take action in response to events in circumstances which were less than ideal. Whether this means that Fox was no more than an opportunist is debatable, but what is certain is that he acted as a practising politician, not a naive idealist. After Fox's death Grenville and Grey appeared both opportunistic and unrealistic, both oversubtle and lamentably foolish, neither high-principled nor politically astute. They were forced to drop their proposals. But George III was determined to drive home his advantage, just as he had done with Pitt in 1801. He tried to extort from his ministers a promise never to raise the Catholic issue again. Grenville and Grey refused to submit to the King's demands. George III then dismissed them and turned to Portland to form a ministry.

Grenville and Grey liked to see themselves as the victims of the King's obstinacy and prejudice, but they had brought ruin upon themselves. Their political judgement had been defective, and they had been inept and tactless in dealing with the King. The truth was that they were not sorry to leave office. Peace had been denied them and victory seemed so remote as to be virtually unthinkable. Their efforts to wage war had been incompetent. Windham, the war secretary, left army recruitment and the provision for an effective home defence force in confusion. Once they were out of office all the Foxites and Grenvillites could do was to criticise their successors, reviving old legends about the influence of the crown, taking a defeatist attitude towards the war, and posing as the friends of enlightenment who had been victimised by a bigoted and reactionary monarch.

Their problems were compounded by the decision in 1807 to dissolve parliament, the King and his new ministers appealing for a vote of confidence from the political nation. The results were highly satisfactory for the King and for the new prime minister, Portland. The gains made by the Talents at the general election of 1806 were wiped out. Victory, as usual, had gone to the government of the day. The knowledge that Portland possessed the confidence of the King was the biggest single factor in explaining the result, but the election had been made more complex and more bitter by the issue of 'No Popery'. In the more open constituencies this cry helped to discredit and defeat those who were associated with Grenville and Grey. Once again George III had spoken for the nation in voicing disquiet about a scheme which would have given Catholics partial relief from longstanding disabilities. 'No Popery' was a more popular and more potent cry than parliamentary reform. The Foxites and Grenvillites found it easier to talk of being the victims of blind prejudice, than to concede that they had merely reaped what they had sown. In opposition Grey and Grenville sought to continue to act together, but this was not easy, for as the years went by it became more apparent that only the Catholic question held them together. As for the war, pessimism and gloom constituted their invariable response to virtually every development.

Portland Struggles On

The Portland administration was presided over by a premier who was old and ailing, but it contained Pitt's two most gifted disciples, Canning as foreign secretary and Castlereagh as war secretary. Spencer Perceval, the underrated chancellor of the exchequer, showed resilience and dogged determination, tenacity and skill. Hawkesbury – the future Lord Liverpool – was home secretary. The ministry was, therefore, not without talent. But its early months were blighted by the failure of expeditions inherited from the Talents, and until Napoleon gave his enemies their greatest opportunity for successful resistance by intervening in the domestic politics of Spain and Portugal there was little that the ministry could do but to hang on grimly, in the hope that eventually defiance could earn a suitable reward. Although the Portland ministry represented a coalition of groups which, in varying degrees, looked back to Pitt and to what Pitt was held to represent, it was torn by internal dissension and mutual suspicion. In other words, it was very much like its immediate predecessors. Portland's failure to impose unity upon his ministry and his inability to give a firm lead, or to damp down rivalries which sapped his colleagues' energies, led to much trouble and eventually to dissolution.

Canning was the most brilliant member of the government. Fully conscious of his own gifts, he was impatient with the slowness and indecision of Portland and by what he deemed the sluggish mediocrity which surrounded him. Canning yearned for action. He could be bold and daring, as was shown by the seizure of the Danish fleet at Copenhagen in order to deny it to the French. But Canning was not content to be a member of a team. He longed to lead. But he knew that he would himself be unacceptable as first minister. His sharp tongue and astringent wit had made enemies, both within the ministry and on the floor of the House of Commons. What he needed was a prime minister who would be easily led. Only then would he be able to infuse much-needed energy and direction into the management of affairs. Canning believed that Portland's days were numbered. The Duke was in poor health. Despite his long experience of politics he was no more than a stopgap chief minister. Canning saw Chatham, the elder brother of Pitt, as a possible successor to Portland. He lacked ability, but he had status, and in suitable circumstances he would be acceptable to the majority of the ministers. Since Chatham was also a soldier Canning thought he discerned an opportunity to turn military necessity to political advantage.

Calculations about future political developments were as important as military considerations when a decision came to be made in 1809 about the choice of the military commander of the expedition to Walcheren. The early months of 1809 were difficult for the government. The Duke of York's former mistress, Mrs Anne Clarke, acting in collusion with a raffish radical MP, Colonel G. L. Wardle, publicised alleged instances of corruption in army administration, pointing the finger of responsibility at the Duke himself. York had proved himself a capable military administrator, whatever his limitations as a commander in the field, and he earned his reputation as the soldier's friend by his diligent efforts to improve the lot of the common soldier. Sadly the fuss over Wardle's allegations compelled the Duke of York to resign as commander-in-chief. The British army lost a fine administrator: it was small comfort to the Duke or to the government when both Mrs Clarke and Wardle were later discredited. The controversy over the case enabled the opposition to revive accusations of massive corruption, extensive secret influence, sinister executive power. But Grenville and Grey disliked the way in which radicals such as Burdett and Cartwright made much of the running, and it was all the more galling for them when attacks on corruption came to be mingled with demands for parliamentary reform which went far beyond what any good Whig could possibly approve. Curwen, an independent backbencher, introduced a bill to suppress the sale of parliamentary seats. Shrewdly, Perceval accepted the principle of the bill, and then carried several decisive amendments. It was generally agreed that Curwen's Act marked a diminution in crown influence. Certainly, whenever influence was exercised it had to be more subtly done than simply by holding out crude financial inducements.

While the government had to fend off attacks, Grey and Grenville had just as awkward a time trying to distance themselves from radical extremism. Grey disliked making too much of the Mrs Clarke affair, and although he remained in favour of parliamentary reform in principle he never forgot that the issue divided Grenville and his supporters from those who believed themselves to be in the true Foxite tradition. But no Foxite could approve of universal manhood suffrage, annual parliaments, or the ballot. When Thomas Brand introduced a reform bill in May 1810 he hoped to show that moderate reform meant something far different from the schemes promulgated by Burdett, Cartwright and the radicals. Brand contented himself with triennial parliaments, the enfranchisement of copyholders in the counties and householders paying local taxes in the boroughs, the disfranchisement of decayed boroughs and the redistribution of such seats to more populous areas. He affirmed his willingness to contemplate the offer of compensation to the disfranchised. There was nothing new about Brand's proposals; indeed, they were an echo of those put forward in the 1780s. They were rejected by 234 votes to 115 in the House of Commons. The Foxites generally supported the bill, which was a sign that parliamentary reform was more securely associated with the Foxite tradition than had been the case fifteen or twenty years earlier. Grey himself held aloof. He contented himself by anaemically asserting that parliamentary reform was a wise measure when it was not sought by clamour or advocated by mischief-makers, but soberly requested by the more serious elements in the community. The Grenvillites disliked the proposals; they had not shifted their position on parliamentary reform. Grey was therefore anxious to avoid saying or doing anything which would put the alliance with Grenville under strain. He and Grenville had enough problems without seeking new areas of difficulty. The outcome of Brand's initiative was that the Foxites had the consolation that the reform cause had polled better in the Commons than at any time since Pitt's attempted reform in 1785. They had also done enough to show that extremists and radicals did not, after all, have a monopoly of the reform issue. But their differences with the Grenvillites on the question had been highlighted, as had the related lack of enthusiasm by the leaders of the two main opposition groups. Whatever the vote on Brand's bill indicated for the future of parliamentary reform, it demonstrated that the issue was unlikely to carry any party into government.

Amid all these developments Canning had never lost sight of the political situation which might arise should Portland find it impossible to carry on as head of the government, or should any successor get into difficulties. Meanwhile, Castlereagh had devoted himself with painstaking attention to detail in the tasks facing the war department. He was just as eager as Canning to prepare for a bold stroke which would enable Britain to take the offensive in the war. To achieve this he believed that an expeditionary force should be held in readiness, available for commitment to the Continent whenever and wherever an opportunity presented itself. As part of this design, Castlereagh improved methods of recruitment to the army. He reorganised the local and national militia, seeking to encourage transfers from the militia to the army, and making the militia more efficient by raising the levels of training and providing for the inspection of militia units. When the French intervened in the

Iberian peninsula Castlereagh was quick to see an opportunity to challenge them.

Iberian Opportunities

There was widespread enthusiasm in Britain for the Spanish rising of May 1808. Faced with the imposition of Napoleon's brother Joseph on the throne of Spain the Spaniards rose against the French and their example fired the Portuguese with a similar determination to defy the invader. Napoleon had been compelled by the logic of economic conflict with Britain to intervene in Portugal and Spain. He was seeking to close the ports of Europe to the British by his Berlin and Milan decrees, and once he had settled the affairs of central Europe he was eager to push his reluctant Spanish allies into more wholehearted compliance. But it was one thing to try to bring the evasive Godoy into line, quite another to depose the House of Bourbon in Spain and the House of Braganza in Portugal. Napoleon provoked national risings of the sort which in the previous decade the French had regarded as of assistance to their schemes. Now the Spanish liberals were in an impossible position. They had to chose between hopes of liberal reform from the French, and the pressing demands of the patriotic cause. The majority of Spaniards rallied to King Ferdinand. The Spanish patriots hated the French so much that they looked for aid to their old enemies, the British.

Even the opposition in Britain shared much of the prevalent enthusiasm for the Iberian patriots in their struggle against the French. Lord Holland, Charles James Fox's nephew and the man who, more than any other, was the guardian of his uncle's memory, knew Spain well. He ardently supported the Spanish cause and urged British intervention on Spain's behalf. Sheridan, now nearing the end of a political career which had been marked by much frustration as well as graced by brilliant oratory, spoke eloquently of the valour and glory of the Spanish resistance. As for the disciples of Pitt, they could recall that not long before he had died their revered master had stated that Napoleon would be defeated only when he faced the resistance of a people, and that the country in which this was most likely to happen was Spain. When Spanish envoys arrived in Britain asking for help it seemed right and inevitable to offer them assistance. A British army was despatched to Portugal, and subsidies were promised to the Spaniards. The great Peninsular War had begun.

But the struggle was more protracted than many had expected. It had been fondly imagined that victory would soon crown the efforts of the Spaniards and Portuguese. The strength of Spanish armies was habitually exaggerated, the potential of popular resistance naively inflated. When ambitious hopes were disappointed, and the road to victory proved long and hard, opposition politicians were prompt to lapse into despondency and gloom. Grey and Grenville sympathised with the Spaniards in their struggle, but after Corunna Grenville morosely declared that no British army should ever be recommitted to the Continent, while a few months later Grey looked upon Talavera as a defeat. In comparison with such pessimists, the determination of the ministers to fight on endeared them to the King, whose own health was now failing fast, and to the majority in the House of Commons, who loathed the defeatism of the parliamentary opposition.

The British commitment to the Iberian peninsula had been dogged with controversy from the start. Castlereagh had sent out the expeditionary force under the command of one of his protégés, a fellow-Irishman, Arthur Wellesley, the brother of Lord Wellesley, the former governor-general of India. Wellesley defeated the French at Vimiero, but he was prevented from following up his victory by the caution and hesitancy of his superiors, Dalrymple and Burrard. Worse still, they negotiated an armistice with the French, the notorious Convention of Cintra, which permitted the French to take their loot with them on abandoning Portugal. The retiring French were transported in British ships, but no promise was extorted from them never to serve in the peninsula again. There had been good grounds for an armistice. It ensured the evacuation of Portugal by the French and this was no unworthy achievement. But in Britain the terms were denounced as a crass and cowardly betrayal of the Spaniards and Portuguese, and the three British generals were recalled to face an inquiry.

At first the government had refused to believe the news about the Convention, but once the agreement's authenticity was established, Castlereagh believed that there was no honourable alternative to observing the terms. Sir John Moore took over the command of the British expeditionary force. Soon he was involved in a bold campaign in northern Spain, risking his army in order to threaten Napoleon's lines of communication and thus draw the French emperor away from the Spaniards. Frustrated by what he regarded as the incompetence of his marshals, Napoleon had intervened personally in Spain, but before he could deal with Moore he was compelled to return to Paris because of the deteriorating diplomatic situation. After a fearful retreat the British defeated the French at the battle of Corunna and the army was successfully evacuated. But Moore himself was killed and the achievements of his campaign were obscured by grief at his death and gloom at the news of another British evacuation. Castlereagh was determined, whatever the factiousness of the opposition, to recommit the British army to Portugal. Wellesley, happily cleared of any responsibility for the Convention of Cintra, returned to take command of the British forces in Portugal. After the risks taken by Moore, Wellesley was instructed that his chief objective was to secure Portugal. Any help he could give the Spaniards would be welcome, but only if Portugal had been secured as a firm base. Unlike Moore, Wellesley believed that Portugal could be denied to the French, although with characteristic caution he did not neglect to make contingency plans for an orderly embarkation should the need arise. In all this he had the support of Castlereagh, but Castlereagh himself was to fall victim to political intrigue, and the Portland ministry was finally to collapse amid derision and disaster.

Walcheren and Disaster

The problems facing Napoleon in Spain had convinced the Austrians that the opportunity had come to challenge Napoleon's dominance in central Europe. Napoleon reacted swiftly to the Austrian threat, defeating the Austrians at the battle of Wagram. Soon he was able to impose yet another peace upon the Austrian emperor and to compel the Habsburgs to become his allies, however reluctantly they did so. By marrying the Archduchess Marie Louise, Napoleon hoped to establish his dynasty and cement the Austrian alliance. The British government had been anxious to assist the Austrians, just as they had sought to help the Spaniards and the Portuguese. Inevitably their attention was drawn to the Low Countries. Despite the battle of Trafalgar Napoleon had not given up all hope of invading England. He retained a large fleet of transports in the mouth of the River Scheldt; should the opportunity arise, he would be ready to exploit it. The British believed that they could combine a blow against French shipping with a diversionary action which would draw off French forces from the Austrian campaign. Castlereagh threw his considerable powers of concentration into planning an amphibious assault, initially on the island of Walcheren. Although he was aware of the dangers of disease he hoped that by supplying adequate provisions, the right type of clothing, and sensible advice on diet and hygiene, the risks of disease could be minimised. The prospect of seizing Antwerp exercised a powerful attraction for the British government, as the ministers tried to envisage how they could aid the Austrians and challenge Napoleon's hegemony in the Low Countries.

The Walcheren expedition also gave Canning his chance to push forward Chatham. Nothing could enhance Chatham's claims to be considered as a possible successor to Portland more than a sensationally successful military exploit. Canning therefore pressed for Chatham's appointment as commander of the military forces involved in the expedition to Walcheren. But the plan failed. The assault took so long to mount that it came too late effectively to help the Austrians, and after initial successes the British forces became bogged down on the island of Walcheren – which was precisely what the campaign's exponents had wanted to avoid. Strachan, the naval commander, was at odds with Chatham, whom he regarded as dilatory and indecisive. The casualty rate, chiefly from disease, was appalling. Eventually the British withdrew. What had been intended to be an incisive stroke became a lingering catastrophe. The blow to government morale was grievous, and the opposition made the most of the opportunity to denounce ministerial incompetence. Canning, now eager to distance himself from Chatham, sought to cast upon Castlereagh the chief responsibility for failure and thus identify a scapegoat for disaster. Portland could not bring himself to act. When Castlereagh heard about a proposed government reshuffle, which involved his own demotion, he felt wronged and betrayed. He believed that his colleagues had behaved deceitfully and that Canning in particular had plotted his downfall in an underhand fashion. To the horror of the King, Castlereagh fought a duel with Canning. Portland had a stroke. Amid confusion and rancour the ministry dissolved. But not to the advantage of the opposition: Grey and Grenville were in no sense an alternative ministry, patiently waiting in the wings. Spencer Perceval, quiet, determined, fired by intense religious conviction and able to win the confidence of the House of Commons by his competence and lack of ostentation set about restoring the situation.

Perceval Rallies the Nation

Perceval was denied the services of Canning and Castlereagh, both of whom had to do penance on the backbenches. Camden, Westmorland,

and Eldon carried on. Bathurst became foreign secretary, though soon he was succeeded by the Marquis Wellesley. Liverpool became war secretary, thus adding the third of the secretaryships of state to the offices he had held. Although frequently derided as weak, second-rate, lacking in imagination and deficient in flair, the Perceval administration laid the foundations for victory. This was not immediately apparent to contemporaries. There seemed little for the government to do, other than manfully struggle on. But Liverpool proved an admirable successor to Castlereagh as war secretary. He loyally supported the British army in Portugal. Castlereagh's improved schemes of recruitment had created the armies with which to fight. Liverpool showed a consistent and intelligent grasp of the long-term strategic issues.

At home the ministry faced a grim prospect. Napoleon's continental system had been thwarted, but it nevertheless did much damage to British trade. There was much distress, highlighted by the Luddite riots in the Midlands. Perceval was conscious of the wisdom of broadening his basis of support. In April 1812 he brought Sidmouth into the government. Canning once said that Sidmouth was like the measles: everyone had to have him once. But Sidmouth brought sober sense and sound judgement together with valuable support in the House of Commons. Sidmouth appealed to those who distrusted men of genius and preferred sobriety to brilliance. He was not fitted to lead, but he was admirably equipped to serve in any administration. Perceval even approached the opposition, but he failed to persuade either Grey or Grenville to join him. His overture had been sincere. The war was the greatest single issue; it reduced everything else to the level of a minor disagreement. But the memory of past experiences led Grenville and Grey to refuse to serve. Perhaps they were hoping for great things when George III died, but their relations with the Prince of Wales were under strain. Grey got on particularly badly with the Prince. But when George III became ill – and this time his incapacity was to be permanent – the opposition had looked with expectancy to the Prince, treasuring high hopes of what he might do for them as regent.

It was ironic that in 1811 Grenville opposed a Regency Bill which in all essentials was closely modelled on that which he had dutifully supported in 1788. Pitt had claimed that a limited regency ought to be provided for by act of parliament; Perceval followed the Pittite precedent. The Prince of Wales was to be regent, but his powers regarding the appointment and dismissal of ministers and the distribution of peerages and patronage were to be restricted for twelve months. Nevertheless the

Grenvillites looked for some change in the Regent's choice of ministers. But neither Grenville nor Grey could make up their differences with Lord Moira and those who were regarded as the Prince's own party. Although the Prince would have liked some of his old friends to enter the ministry, he had no wish to change the direction of government policy. He believed in fighting the war to a victorious conclusion and he was proud of the performance of the British army in Portugal and Spain. Grenville and Grey rejected joining the ministry on Perceval's terms. The Prince was annoyed by their petulant and proud refusal. The failure to win over Grey and Grenville led to the ministry being strengthened in other ways. Castlereagh returned to office as foreign secretary. With both Sidmouth and Castlereagh in the government, Perceval had thwarted Canning and the proud and ambitious Wellesley. He had failed to divide Grey and Grenville, but it was clear that Perceval had established a firm command over his administration, and this coincided with signs that the tide of battle was beginning to flow in Britain's favour.

1812 was the decisive year. In Spain, Wellington won one of his most brilliant victories at Salamanca – 'forty thousand men defeated in forty minutes' – and for a brief period he liberated Madrid. Napoleon was immersed in his disastrous Russian campaign. Britain had to endure the irritating distraction of a war with the United States, brought about partly by American resentment of Britain's assertion of the right of search at sea and partly by the ambitions of those Americans who still cast an envious eye on Canada. Sadly, Perceval did not live to see the culmination of much that he had toiled hard to achieve. In May 1812 he was shot by a businessman with an imagined grievance. Liverpool succeeded as first minister; but, before he could establish his administration, he had to face a crisis brought about by the success of a backbench resolution calling upon the Prince Regent to provide himself with an efficient government. Behind the resolution lay the naive desire of many MPs for an all-party administration, but broadening the government could only mean making a bid for the support of the opposition Grey and Grenville groups, and for a brief time it looked as if Liverpool's ministry would end before it could prove itself in office. But the Prince Regent no longer wished to summon Grey and Grenville to assume the major responsibility for the direction of public policy. Amid bewilderment and recrimination, he decided that there was no practicable alternative to Liverpool.

Grey and Grenville accepted their exclusion from office as final proof of the apostasy of the Prince Regent. The truth was that they had missed their chance two-and-a-half years earlier. Now they refused to abandon their advocacy of Catholic relief, perhaps because it was one of the few issues on which they were fully agreed. The Prince Regent regarded them as dangerously unsound on that issue and on the war in Spain. Although he had used both Wellesley and Moira as intermediaries, he was determined not to yield on either the Catholic question or the prosecution of the war. He outwitted his former friends, establishing conditions which meant that while Liverpool carried on, Catholic relief remained an open question within the administration. The Prince Regent had no qualms about the determination of the Liverpool ministry to fight the war with complete commitment to outright victory. The episode illustrated how decisive the attitudes of the Prince Regent were. The opposition paid a high price for alienating him. It was all the more galling for Grey and Grenville, in that they could boast about 150 supporters in the House of Commons. Singly they were the most numerous of the parliamentary factions. This gave a spurious credibility to their belief that only double-dealing had kept them out of office. But the truth was that they could not hope to attain office without the confidence of the crown and a willingness to reach acceptable compromises with other political groups. They had lost the Prince Regent's goodwill and they were palpably incapable of reaching agreement with other interested parties.

It was all the more infuriating for Grey and Grenville when Liverpool strengthened his position by calling a general election in September 1812. His supporters in the Commons increased by about 60. The political nation had given retrospective approval to the actions taken by the Prince Regent to keep the opposition out of office. But although Liverpool had recovered from an uncertain start, his prospects were far from bright. The war dragged on. Although 1812 proved to be the turning-point, this was less obvious to contemporaries than to those with the advantage of hindsight. Napoleon's powers of recovery seemed astonishing. Britain was enduring considerable economic distress. The pressures of war and the onset of new technology combined to disrupt trade and throw men out of work. In the Midlands the Luddite disturbances highlighted the difficulties and tribulations of the hour. Liverpool had to establish his ministry, retain the confidence of the Prince Regent, broaden his support in the Commons whenever the opportunity for doing so presented itself, and fend off the criticisms of those carping politicians disappointed in their hopes of place or frustrated by the futilities of opposition. Liverpool had the advantage that public opinion tended to see the opposition as factious and petty-minded, Grey and Grenville being as proud and as vain as they were self-centred. After the abortive negotiations of 1812 there was general agreement that the opposition Whigs were unfit for office. But Liverpool and his colleagues still had to prove that they could rise to the challenges of war. Only if they were equal to the awesome task of defeating Napoleon would they be able to win the confidence of the House of Commons and of the political nation on more than an interim basis.

4

THE PITTITE TRADITION RENEWED AND EXTENDED

Liverpool and his Ministry

For many years Lord Liverpool was reviled as a mediocrity. Liberals and radicals denounced him as the author of repression at home and the collaborator with reaction abroad. Victorian Tories preferred to look back to Pitt as the true precursor of Tory democracy and to see in George Canning the legitimate heir to Pitt, the lost leader who would have saved Toryism from the taint of reaction, had he been given an earlier opportunity to hold the highest office, or if he had not been struck down so unexpectedly so soon after achieving the premiership. Over the last fifty years, however, the appreciation of Liverpool as a politician has become more sympathetic and more perceptive. No longer is he seen as a fumbling and cautious premier. While his fairmindedness cannot be doubted, it is evident that he exercised a considerable degree of authority within the cabinet. Although he sustained his colleagues, and gave to them a judicious degree of freedom in handling the affairs of their departments, he nevertheless determined the overall thrust of government policy. His ministry was also richly endowed with talent. Among the older men Sidmouth and Eldon were central in the maintenance of the ministry's credibility. Castlereagh and Canning were to be of signal importance in the House of Commons as well as in the direction of foreign policy. Among the younger men there were several who were to be prime ministers when their own time came: Robinson, Peel, Palmerston and Aberdeen, while Canning and Wellington served as first ministers in the years immediately after Liverpool's death. The ministry was certainly not a collection of nonentities. On the contrary, while being comprehensive in its range of political viewpoints, it had its full share of men of strong opinions, administrative capacity, political determination and personal resilience. But the personality of Liverpool was decisive for the ministry's longevity, harmony, and ability to function so effectively for so long.

Liverpool came to the premiership with ample political experience behind him. He had entered politics early. As a young man he had witnessed the fall of the Bastille. Although it would be foolish to trace all later political responses to that overwhelming experience there is no doubt that he never lost a distrust for popular movements and a hatred for demagogy and violence. During the long years of war he had held the most important offices of state. He had been foreign secretary, home secretary and war secretary. His demeanour appealed strongly to back-bench MPs but, after succeeding his father as second Earl of Liverpool, he sat in the Lords and had therefore to rely on others to maintain control of the House of Commons. As war secretary he had been fully committed to the Peninsular War and this had certainly endeared him to the Prince Regent. As a young man he had been diffident and shy, overshadowed by more brilliant talents such as those of his friend, George Canning. But the maturing effect of political experience, the responsibilities of office, and the trust and respect of older politicians enabled a quiet confidence and an unfussy dependability to become familiar features of Liverpool's political style. He valued the views and opinions of others, but he did not shrink from hard decisions. As was fitting in a Pittite, he had due reverence for the status and powers of the crown, but he was determined not to allow the waywardness of the Prince Regent to distort or frustrate government policy. He made no attempt to cramp the legitimate freedom of conviction or conscience deemed appropriate for his colleagues, but he pursued agreed object-ives with steady dedication and without false heroics. Ministers con-ducted the business of their departments in their own way, but they were to conform to the general principles upon which the government had agreed. The Catholic question remained open throughout the ministry's long life. There was no other way of dealing with it, since some ministers were as deeply committed to resisting Catholic relief as others were pledged to it. Similarly, Liverpool recognised the limits within which he had to work in dealing with the House of Commons. He did not command backbench support; he could only appeal to the integrity of members, seeking to persuade rather than to tyrannise. All he asked of MPs, and all he could dare to ask, was a generally favourable disposition. He knew that it was unrealistic and politically indiscreet to ask for more. Although he was in some respects the heir to Pitt, he had to work hard to strengthen the roots of parliamentary support for his ministry. He was, therefore, always eager to win the confidence of new groups within the Commons. He neglected no opportunity to convert hesitant approval into committed approbation. As the political climate changed he was willing to overlook old disagreements in order to achieve present cooperation. He held no grudges and he displayed no malice.

It is difficult to find the right designation to define Liverpool's political stance. It is far from satisfactory to call Liverpool a Tory. Although the word was beginning to be used as a convenient means of separating supporters of the Pittite tradition from the opposition groups of Grey and Grenville, who had by a curiously successful sleight of hand appropriated the term Whig, it no longer possessed the resonances which had once been associated with Toryism: divine right, passive obedience, or a sentimental affection for the king-over-the-water. In most matters pertaining to the institutions of government Liverpool was conservative. Like most Englishmen of his time he believed the constitution to be unique and that its continued security was the greatest safeguard for the wellbeing of the nation. But Liverpool was not a reactionary. In some ways he was sympathetic to the new thinking of the age on commercial and economic affairs, though it would be misleading to interpret his response to ideas of freer trade in too ideological or intellectual a fashion. Like many politicians he was adept at tacking new ideas on to what was a rather old-fashioned set of basic assumptions. What he valued was the likelihood of practicable improvement. He was prepared to borrow ideas or policies from any source if they held out the prospect of tangible benefit without jeopardising traditional institutions or inherited liberties. He was cautious and pragmatic, and he was shrewd enough to realise that modest concession and carefully implemented adjustment were the price to be paid for stability and continuity.

Liverpool believed that the alliance of church and state had been one reason for the nation's prosperity since the Glorious Revolution of 1688. He was uneasy about admitting Catholics to public office without restriction. He knew that Catholic emancipation was the most dangerous issue so far as the survival of his ministry was concerned. He was prepared to make some concessions, short of full emancipation, such as enfranchising Catholic freeholders or admitting Catholics to the magistracy, but he knew how vulnerable he was on the Catholic issue. He had no wish to appear to make concessions to agitation or popular pressure, particularly in

Ireland. Throughout his ministry he had no choice but to insist that the Catholic question remained open. Not only did his government contain supporters and opponents of relief, but within each camp there was a range of attitudes which defied simple categorisation, just as the Catholic issue cut across conventional political alignments. For most of the years during which Liverpool was prime minister, Catholic emancipation was a much more divisive and sensitive issue than parliamentary reform. And, above everything else, Liverpool was determined to keep his ministry in being. He disliked politicians who placed devotion to any dogma or to any faction before service to the crown; every politician of good will had a duty to subordinate personal preferences to the national good. His colleagues knew that Liverpool would behave honourably, that he respected their own convictions and their judgement, but they also knew that he regarded loyalty and devotion to the public service as the first qualification for any minister. Personal ambition and private pique were likely to cause dissension and to aggravate discontent. These were an inevitable but regrettable feature of political life: Liverpool did all he could to diminish their potency for evil within his administration.

Liverpool knew that if he went too far ahead of conventional opinion he risked rejection by the majority of backbenchers in the Commons. Whenever he sought to take a new initiative he had to do so in such a fashion as to reassure the conventionally-minded that nothing too risky was being attempted. Liverpool viewed politics in sober and realistic terms. He recognised that, for much of the time, politicians were reacting to circumstances which they did not control, and dealing with situations which they had neither desired nor created. Even in the midst of controversy, Liverpool retained respect because he obviously moved in the same political world as the men whose support he needed to survive in the fragile arena of regency politics.

Yet, although he was no doctrinaire innovator, some things did change during his fifteen-year premiership. Few historians would now see this as stemming entirely from a dramatic breach with the past in 1821–22. The old suggestion that the ministry may be divided into two periods, a period of reaction to about 1822 and an era of liberalism thereafter, is simplistic and misleading. Liverpool did not see his ministry changing course or shedding one set of convictions for another. All that was happening was that a stronger emphasis could be placed on several assumptions which had been present from the start. Broadly speaking, Liverpool faced three challenges during his premiership.

First, there was the obvious challenge of winning the war against Napoleon; secondly, there was the problem of adapting to the coming of peace when the economy was facing intense difficulties and when the impact of distress seemed to have potentially dangerous implications; and thirdly, there was the task in the 1820s of sustaining the commercial growth which had become a marked feature of the period, just when the disappearance of the much-feared and greatly exaggerated Jacobin threat made opinion less inclined to plump for safety first. Reform became a popular cry in the 1820s, but in part this was a reflection of Liverpool's success in winning the war and in seeing-off real or imagined Jacobinical violence. Like many governments which survive for a long time, Liverpool's ministry faced problems in its latter years which were to some extent the consequences of success. But the problems which Liverpool faced on taking office were so formidable that few guessed that Liverpool's premiership would be either lengthy or successful.

Without the confidence of the Prince Regent, Liverpool could not have survived. Here one of his greatest difficulties was that while the Prince Regent came to share most of his father's prejudices, as he grew older he never attained his father's integrity. The Duke of York was just as reactionary as the Prince Regent, but he was a man of conviction and honesty and in some respects would have been a much easier man for the politicians to deal with. Although the influence of the crown had been in decline since the 1780s the attitudes of the Prince Regent could still be decisive; no account of the period which ignores the crucial part played by the crown in the formation, maintenance and dissolution of ministries is true to the realities of regency politics. The Prince Regent might infuriate or irritate; he might be evasive, dishonest, and unscrupulous; he might shuffle uneasily or dig in his heels, as when he insisted that something should be done about his wife or when he asserted that his conscience would not allow him to contemplate Catholic emancipation; but no premier could ignore him. His freedom of manoeuvre was constrained by the chances he had of finding an alternative first minister, but the prerequisite for political success was still the confidence of the crown. This does not mean that Liverpool was unduly obsequious. He respected the crown more than he respected the person of the Regent. He was willing to tell the Prince Regent in forthright and unambiguous language what his constitutional duties were and what he risked by neglecting them. Liverpool insisted that it was the Prince Regent's duty to give his confidence, without reservations or misgivings, to those ministers who had the support of the Commons. If he lost confidence in them it was then his duty to dismiss them and to send for someone else, rather than intriguing against them or making life difficult for them by ambivalent duplicity or playing one minister off against another. It was hard for the Prince Regent to submit to such instruction, but it was difficult for him to get rid of Liverpool when there was no readily-identifiable alternative. The Prince Regent's antipathy to the opposition Whigs came to be so intense that, however he might grumble about his ministers, he had to accept that he had to continue working with them. When members of the opposition, such as Brougham, flaunted their sympathy for Princess Caroline in a provocative and partisan spirit the Prince Regent loathed them all the more. But his ministers had still to humour him. This led to the government taking initiatives over the Princess of Wales which brought it odium and humiliation. It also gave radicals the opportunity to exploit the scandal of the Prince Regent's detestation of his wife with considerable publicity and rampant malice.

At its inception the government was dominated by Liverpool and those who held the most important offices of state. Eldon as lord chancellor, Sidmouth as home secretary, Castlereagh as foreign secretary, were the key figures. Yet of these only Castlereagh could properly be called a Pittite. Eldon had served under Pitt as solicitor-general and lord chancellor but he had never been wholly identified with Pitt. His robust and often intransigent conservatism meant that on certain issues – of which Catholic relief was the most significant – he had been staunchly opposed to Pitt. Eldon had first served as lord chancellor under Addington. He always showed a tough independency of mind and he saw his main duty as the defence of the constitution against every threat. Similarly, Sidmouth may be described as conservative, but throughout his career he had been prepared to collaborate, with varying degrees of enthusiasm and success, with Pitt, Fox, Grenville and Portland. Sidmouth's opposition to Catholic emancipation separated him from those who believed themselves to be the heirs of Pitt, while his cautious approach to the means and methods of waging war earned him the disdain of those, such as Canning, who believed that a vigorous prosecution of the war was an intrinsic feature of the Pittite creed. But Sidmouth was not the negligible figure denounced by Canning and so often deplored by later generations of historians. He may have been a second-rank politician rather than a man of transcendent abilities, but he was more judicious and less erratic than many of his critics; for that reason many MPs had initially rejoiced at his appointment as prime minister in 1801. His presence in government under Liverpool was reassuring. Sidmouth's common sense and capacity to assess what backbench feeling was likely to be assured him of a major role in the government. Eldon and Sidmouth have so often been branded as reactionaries that it is easy to overlook the fact that in many of their convictions and in much of their behaviour they represented the mainstream of opinion within the political nation. Their presence in the ministry was seen as a pledge of its sanity and soundness and a guarantee of its competence.

Castlereagh was a very different figure. He had owed much to the patronage of Pitt, but however mercurial his rise he had always been controversial, whether as Irish secretary or war secretary. Yet his performance of his duties had always been exemplary. He had the vision to see broad issues and the tenacity to handle minute detail. His ability to shoulder an immense workload was formidable. But there were those who regarded him with reserve, partly because he was an Irishman, partly because his duel with Canning had hinted at an intensity of feeling and a sensitivity which his habitual courtesy and self-control usually hid from the public. As foreign secretary Castlereagh masterminded the final grand coalition which brought about the downfall of Napoleon. His determination to involve Britain in Europe was distrusted, chiefly because it was misunderstood. He also acted as leader of the House of Commons. Since the prime minister was in the Lords it was essential that the leadership of the House of Commons was in trustworthy hands. Castlereagh was no orator in the classical mould. Wellington once said of him that he could do anything except make a speech in the House of Commons. This was less than fair, and not wholly accurate: as a young man Castlereagh had made his mark in the Irish House of Commons, no mean feat in an assembly famous for its eloquence. He often spoke good sense, even if his metaphors were mixed and his syntax clumsy. His real gifts in dealing with the Commons lay in his tact and understanding when bargaining with backbenchers. He was a master of the art of negotiation, not only at the level of international diplomacy but also in the testing intimacy of the House of Commons. His reputation for courtesy, integrity and fair play endeared him to those who had little grasp of the sophisticated assumptions underlying his foreign policy. Liverpool knew that Castlereagh had a decisive contribution to make to the survival of the ministry. He therefore resisted suggestions that Castlereagh should relinquish the leadership of the House of Commons. This put a great strain on Castlereagh, a strain which undoubtedly contributed to his mental breakdown and suicide in 1822. He was a much more influential figure in the Commons than Vansittart, the chancellor of the exchequer. Nevertheless, not even Castlereagh could ensure that the ministry would be free from embarrassment in the House of Commons.

The reason for this was that Liverpool was not in the position of a modern prime minister, who can rely on party discipline to maintain an obedient majority in the Commons on all major issues. Too often historians have written of the two-party system in Britain in ways which read back into the past the patterns of behaviour and the standards of conduct which were really the product of the second half of the nineteenth century. To assume that all MPs were 'Whig' or 'Tory' in a sense which predetermined their response to events or their attitudes towards the governments of the day is to ignore the complex and frequently confusing realities of early nineteenth-century politics. Although by the 1820s many MPs were willing in a general sense to think of themselves as offering or withholding support from the government this did not mean that they identified their political future with the success or failure of a single political group. Similarly, to discern a 'Whig' or 'Tory' ideology, working itself out through a predictable pattern of political behaviour, is to impose too rational and too distinct an alignment upon often incoherent or instinctive modes of conduct. Although hallowed by tradition and made familiar by habitual use, Whig and Tory were not the most enlightening terms for assisting an understanding of the rivalries of those seeking office or a comprehension of the assumptions with which the active politicians approached the issues of the day.

Fox and his followers had claimed to be the true representatives of the Whig tradition. For too long this presumption has been taken at its face value. Fox and his friends had no monopoly of Whig thinking. Pitt's basic assumptions were all Whig, as were those of the men who, during the long years of war, believed they were defending the constitution against the threat of Jacobinism and the dangers of domestic unrest. Such a stance was conservative, but its ideology derived from those Whig assumptions which had been dominant throughout the eighteenth century. Because the Foxites asserted that they were the true Whigs, and because Tory was held to mean whatever was the opposite of what was Whig, it was assumed that Pitt or Burke or Portland could be deemed Tories by way of contrast. Yet their presuppositions about liberty and property and the balanced constitution and representation were all Whig, and Burke had seen himself as appealing from the new to the old Whigs by way of exposing the fallacies and dangers which he had believed to be implicit in Fox's expressed sympathy for the French

Revolution. Many conservatives believed that Fox had departed from Whig principles. There was, in fact, no purity in ideology. Much of what passed for ideological debate was a squabble between various schools of Whig as to how the Whig tradition was to be properly understood and how it was to be politically applied in the situation created by the French Revolution.

Nor was there any purity of development in party terms. The party of Grey and Grenville was an uneasy coalition. Since the 1780s the opposition Whigs had in reality consisted of a series of alliances. First, there had been the alliance of North and Fox, with the Northites either fading from the scene or moving away from Fox in the aftermath of the catastrophe of 1784. Then Fox had suffered the loss of Portland and conservative Whigs in 1794. In the years 1801 to 1804 Fox and Grenville had been drawn together by a common opposition to Addington and a devotion to the cause of Catholic emancipation. Finally, during the Ministry of All the Talents, Fox and Grenville had drawn other groups, of which that led by Sidmouth had been the most significant, into temporary alliance. With the defeat of the Talents, and the defection of the Sidmouthites, Grey and Grenville struggled hard to maintain an alliance which was inspired by sheer desperation. Though they were of one mind on the Catholic question they often differed over the war, despite a common pessimism which came to the fore from time to time. On parliamentary reform Grenville remained hostile, while Grey was uneasy about any agitation of the subject which might embarrass Grenville and lead to the breakdown of the opposition coalition. Grey liked to think that the future of English politics lay with an opposition which was loyal to the Foxite tradition, but he had little inclination to take any action which might taint the opposition with too strong an association with radicalism. It is one of the ironies of history that such a futile opposition, whose character had been determined as much by the pressures of survival as by principle or conviction, should be seen either as a coherent party or as the most faithful custodian of Whig principles.

Just as the opposition party was a curious coalition, which Grey and Grenville strove hard to maintain against those forces which threatened to drive them apart, so Liverpool's Tory party was in reality an alliance of various groups, united in the defence of the establishment and in calling for the vigorous prosecution of the war, but finely shaded by private preferences and the power of personal affinities. Liverpool had to build up a broadly-based coalition, made up of those who looked back to Pitt, and of those who were patriotic and conservative but who hesitated to call themselves Pittites in anything other than the vaguest of senses. The ministers never lost the memory of old rivalries and they did not disguise continuing disagreements. The war gave the appearance of simplicity to a political situation which was intricate and subtle, volatile and unpredictable. Many of those who were prepared to give general support to Liverpool because he held out the prospect of a reasonably stable ministry retained the right to criticise, obstruct or even defeat the administration on any issue which threatened essential interests or habitual loyalties. Throughout his premiership, therefore, Liverpool was on the alert for the best means of extending the range of his support, or of acquiring one faction as an insurance against the loss or weakening of another. The Liverpool ministry was not the creation of a party nor was it the natural outcome of a fully functioning party system. It would be more truthful to say that throughout his premiership Liverpool was engaged in the creation of a party. In invoking the shade of Pitt, whether over the conduct of the war, in the defence of national institutions, in the reduction of customs duties, or the relaxation of commercial regulations, Liverpool was seeking to do more than revive a tradition or reinvigorate a party. He was using the legacy of the past in order to accomplish and then sustain a broadly-based following which would enable him to cope with the challenges of the present. His political objectives were dictated by the priorities of office and the demands of power. In every appeal to the various factions in the Commons, and to the sentiments of the House in general, he was motivated by the traditional need to win that degree of acceptance by a majority of MPs which was necessary for survival.

Doctrine was as uncongenial to Liverpool as party organisation. As a minister he lacked the resources of patronage available to his eighteenth-century predecessors, and the techniques of party discipline and management which were to be exploited by his successors later in the nineteenth century. This explains his legendary ambivalence and the fact that the party built up by Liverpool did not long survive his retirement. Only Liverpool's combination of skills could maintain such a comprehensive and so vulnerable an alliance for so long. Only a minister who had his qualities of insight, discretion and tact could strike the right balance between continuity and the need for cautious adjustment to change. Nor was his ministry composed of aristocrats representing the ancient lineage of the country. Most of Liverpool's colleagues had their origins among the country gentry or among the professions or in commerce or manufacture, despite the presence of so many of the ministry's leading figures in the House of Lords. Liverpool's own father had been a professional servant of the crown, Sidmouth's a country doctor, Eldon's a coal merchant, while Castlereagh's roots lay in the mercantile gentry of Ulster. It was well-known that Grey looked down on his opponents as men of dubious birth and doubtful social status. He believed that since they lacked the breeding necessary to stand up to the King or the Regent it was all the more credible that such men should be the agents of royal influence, the tools of corruption, posing a threat to liberties at home and freedoms abroad. However nonsensical such accusations were as an explanation of the frustrations of the opposition, they performed a necessary function in soothing the susceptibilities of Grey and Grenville. But if rank and status were the tests of a government's credibility and character there was a sense in which Liverpool's administration had a distinctly down-to-earth look.

It is possible to regard Liverpool and his colleagues as professional politicians, in that they took their duties seriously and acquired over a period of time a degree of expertise which was impressive by the standards of the age. But even here such terminology may be misleading. They were not in politics to make a career in the modern fashion. Nor did they make vast amounts of money out of the public service. They saw their first duty as carrying on public business within the context of the service of the crown. Possibly they brought to government something of the outlook of civil servants; but, having said that, it must be remembered that the resources of government available to Liverpool were pitiably inadequate, judged by twentieth-century criteria. The administrative machine was rudimentary. The home secretary and the foreign secretary composed their own despatches and did much of the routine work which was later the responsibility of permanent officials. The role of government was still limited, as it had been in Pitt's time, to the handling of public finance, the conduct of foreign relations, the maintenance of public order – though even here the chief responsibility lay with the local magistrates. Expectations of government were dominated by the great issues of war and defence. Legislative programmes were not the means by which governments implemented their policies. When Liverpool and Sidmouth claimed that most of the matters which affected the daily life of the common people lay outside the scope of any government's competence they were recognising elementary truths, as well as giving voice to contemporary assumptions. They believed that the more governments intervened, or sought to intervene, in questions of trade or commerce or manufacture, the less likely it would be that they would do so in a manner which would bring benefits to the people. Such assumptions indicate the gap between the experience and perception of the early nineteenth century and much of the experience and conventional wisdom of the twentieth century.

Final Victory

Once Liverpool had established himself in office in 1812, the most urgent issue facing his administration was the conduct of the war. Hostilities were in a crucial phase because of Napoleon's invasion of Russia. Liverpool knew that the French could be defeated only with the collaboration of effective European allies. Napoleon's Russian campaign held out great possibilities for a new coalition against the French emperor. Castlereagh fully appreciated the opportunities created by Napoleon's defeat in Russia. But he also recognised the anxieties which made Austria and Prussia hold back. They had suffered too much and been defeated too often to take the risk of a precipitate or hasty resort to arms. Here the British commitment to the Iberian peninsula bore rich fruit. In 1812 Wellington had won a brilliant victory over Marmont at Salamanca and had liberated Madrid. Allied success in Spain reminded other Europeans that Napoleon could be thwarted. For four years the French had been implicated in Spain and Portugal. Despite many victories over the Spanish armies they had become bogged down in cruel and relentless guerilla warfare. They had failed to drive the British out of Portugal, which remained a sure base for British operations in Spain. Although at the close of the 1812 campaign Wellington had once again to withdraw to Portugal, Liverpool never doubted the meaning and the potential of the Iberian conflict. He and Castlereagh were fully alert to every opportunity to exploit French reverses and to put localised success in Spain to wider diplomatic purposes.

Napoleon's defeat in Russia led to Prussia changing sides and joining the Russians as allies. But for a time Austria hesitated to commit herself to the struggle against Napoleon. Metternich hoped that Austria might act as an honest-broker. He distrusted Russian and Prussian designs in eastern and central Europe as much as he loathed French dominance in western Europe. But he was reluctant to take up arms – always a hazardous gamble when facing a foe of Napoleon's calibre – without exhausting every possibility of a diplomatic solution. As so often in the past diplomacy held out the best prospect for securing Austrian interests.

But Napoleon's intransigence settled the matter. He rejected every offer of a negotiated peace, shocking Metternich by his indifference to suffering and his obstinate refusal to see the virtues of compromise. Austria finally joined the coalition. Britain was committed to sustaining the allies by generous subsidies as well as by her own efforts in Spain and on the high seas. In 1813 Wellington drove the French out of Spain, winning a dramatic victory at Vittoria. In Germany the war turned inexorably against Napoleon. Yet even after the battle of Leipzig he showed prodigious powers of recovery and resilience. It needed all of Castlereagh's skill in diplomacy to stiffen the determination of the allies. The invasion of France inspired Napoleon to a final display of military brilliance, but he was overwhelmed by the sheer determination of his foes and the exhaustion of France and abdicated in April 1814. In the south of France Wellington defeated Soult and occupied Toulouse before the news of Napoleon's abdication arrived. For want of any better alternative the allies agreed to the restoration of the Bourbons in France, Louis XVIII proving the least objectionable of the possible successors to Napoleon.

Britain had also become involved in war with the United States. The war proved inconclusive. The American invasion of Canada failed. Although the Americans won several famous fights between frigates, the British restored their overall naval supremacy. The British sacked Washington; the Americans defeated and killed Pakenham at the battle of New Orleans. The orders in council, ostensibly one of the main causes of the war, had been revoked before the fighting began. Castlereagh was eager for a settlement with the Americans. He went to great lengths to make a conciliatory peace possible. The Treaty of Ghent ended the war in December 1814. Each side returned to the other whatever it had gained. Once the war with Napoleon was over, there was no need for Britain to insist on the right of search at sea which had so angered American merchants. But the British were just as determined to do nothing which could be interpreted as a possible abandonment of her maritime rights. Castlereagh worked hard to improve Anglo-American relations after the close of a war whose chief legacy was one of mutual resentment and futility. Unlike most other British politicians, Castlereagh appreciated both the potential strength of the United States and the positive value of good Anglo-American relations. More than any of his predecessors as foreign secretary he recognised the significance of American independence for the conduct of British policy in the New World.

Castlereagh and Foreign Policy

The problems of peace in Europe were settled in congress at Vienna. After a generation of war the powers hoped to agree a settlement which would restrict France to her ancient limits, strengthen the states on her borders, and give some hope for security against any possible resurgence of French aggression. But the victors were also seeking due reward for their sacrifices, and soon it became apparent that Britain, Austria and France had much in common by way of checking Russian and Prussian power in central Europe, whatever the quarrels of the previous twenty years. Although Napoleon's escape from Elba, and the subsequent adventure of the hundred days, raised fears that he might re-establish himself as ruler of France, the battle of Waterloo ended what for most European diplomats was an ominous nightmare. France was punished to the extent of being restricted to her 1790 frontiers instead of those of 1792. She also had to pay an indemnity and submit to an army of occupation. But the allies were sufficiently aware of the ambivalence with which many Frenchmen regarded Louis XVIII and the restored monarchy to recognise that a punitive peace would be counterproductive. Throughout the negotiations at Vienna Castlereagh followed the guidelines which he had inherited from his mentor, Pitt. In addition to limiting France to her old boundaries and strengthening the countries adjacent to her, these called for the creation of some method of international consultation which would make the resumption of war between the major powers less likely. Castlereagh believed that Napoleon had been defeated only because the powers had united against him. He therefore hoped that regular congresses, by which threats to peace could be scrutinised and removed, would prevent tense situations developing to the point of war. He was not concerned with setting up anything similar to the League of Nations or the United Nations. Nor was he contemplating a united Europe. In his cautious, pragmatic way he was trying to learn from the experience of wartime cooperation and thus make it possible for the peace settlement to be maintained and adjusted by international collaboration. Castlereagh did not regard the peace as wholly unchangeable. He knew that clashes of interest would occur and that modifications of the peace settlement would become necessary with the passage of time. He hoped that the powers would see that they had a common interest in the preservation of peace, and that by judicious consultation the balance of power could be sustained in such a way as to perpetuate equilibrium in Europe. Castlereagh saw the balance of power chiefly in terms of the relationships between sovereign states. He did not desire, and he was never to condone, collective intervention in the internal affairs of European countries.

Here he came into increasing conflict with Metternich, who believed that the security of the Habsburg empire depended upon preventing liberalism and nationalism manifesting themselves anywhere in Europe. Although Metternich eventually exploited the Holy Alliance for his own ends he had originally acceded to it only to humour Tsar Alexander I, whose brainchild it was. The Tsar's dream of the sovereigns of Europe regarding each other as brothers and treating their subjects with Christian benevolence struck the world-weary diplomats of Europe as ludicrous nonsense, but the Tsar was too powerful and too unpredictable for him not to be flattered. Even Castlereagh, who made no secret of his conviction that the Holy Alliance was a piece of sublime mysticism and nonsense, contemplated keeping the Tsar happy by permitting the Prince Regent to avow his support in a personal capacity. Liverpool insisted that such a gesture was foreign to the spirit of the constitution. More significantly, such a response might well have proved politically embarrassing. Liverpool had no wish to lose the goodwill of the House of Commons for what he considered an empty piece of pretentious folly. He therefore said that the Prince Regent could not accede to the Holy Alliance, though it was reasonable for the Tsar to be told that he was in sympathy with Christian sentiments of brotherhood and benevolence.

Few Englishmen were capable of seeing the difference between the congress system, as advocated by Castlereagh, and the Holy Alliance, as it came to be practised by Metternich, especially in the years after 1818. Canning had always been suspicious of British involvement in Europe. He believed that it was better for Britain to stand aloof from the affairs of the Continent, intervening only when her interests were directly threatened, and then with effect. Castlereagh was convinced that the experience of the previous twenty-five years had shown that Britain was inevitably involved in European questions and that it was better for her to play her part in preventing war than in desperately searching for an ally once war had broken out. But the congress system never worked as Castlereagh hoped it would. Although the Congress of Aix-la-Chapelle was successful in admitting France to the concert of Europe and in ending the allied occupation, subsequent events meant that at Troppau, Laibach and Verona Britain's isolation from her former allies became all the more apparent. By 1821 it was clear that Britain condemned the principle of collective intervention in the internal affairs of sovereign states. Castlereagh had done his best to understand Metternich's point of view, but however much he sympathised with Austria's legitimate concern over developments in Italy he could not condone collective intervention in Naples. It was for Austria to intervene if she believed her interests were threatened by what was happening in the kingdom of the Two Sicilies, but she could not call upon the other powers to engage in collective action unless there was a clear threat to European stability. Britain would not shrink from accepting her responsibilities whenever there was a threat to peace but, unlike Metternich, Castlereagh affirmed that countries were free to develop their domestic institutions in their own way and at their own pace. By the time of Castlereagh's death in August 1822 the congress system was in ruins. It had never been intended to be more than a means of keeping peace in Europe, and it could not be supported by Britain if its purpose was distorted in order to perpetuate the status quo everywhere.

Just as Castlereagh had seen congresses as a security for peace and as a means for adapting the settlement of 1815 to inevitable change, so he had worked hard at Vienna for agreement among the powers for the control and ultimately the suppression of the slave trade. Spain and Portugal regarded British efforts to end the trade in slaves as proof that Britain would stoop to any ruse in order to break into Latin American markets. When the Spaniards experienced trouble with their American colonies, Castlereagh watched the situation carefully. Several years before, at the beginning of the Peninsular War, he had accepted the possible recognition of the independence of the Spanish-American colonies as a means of defending British interests, extending British commerce, and thwarting French ambitions. Now, although he knew that it would be foolish to take any premature step, he once more discerned in the recognition of the Spanish-American republics a real option for Britain. Whatever misgivings he had about hasty constitutional experimentation, he had always regarded the Spanish Bourbons as stupid reactionaries and he had been careful never to condone their domestic policy. Castlereagh saw Spanish liberals as unrealistic and Spanish royalists as intransigent.

While he watched developments in Latin America closely he continued to work patiently to improve British relations with the United States. In the aftermath of the war of 1812 this was not easy. Castlereagh played down the significance of incidents involving American prisoners-of-war and scuffles between British and American seamen at Gibraltar. He was eager for an amicable settlement of the Canadian frontier dispute and of hotly-contested fishing rights in Newfoundland. Although the Oregon question was solved only a quarter of a century after his death, his skill and tact paved the way for a gradual improvement in Anglo-American relations. He was neither condescending nor arrogant in his attitude towards the Americans. He showed his invariable urbanity and courtesy. Like all good negotiators Castlereagh knew how important it was to respect the intelligence and the integrity of those with whom he was treating.

Similarly, he was quick to see the potential dangers created by the Greek revolt in 1820. He differentiated between a general sympathy with the Greeks and ill-considered intervention. He was chiefly concerned with preventing the breakup of the Ottoman empire, believing that the greatest danger to British interests in the Near East came from Russian expansionism. This common anxiety enabled him to cooperate with Metternich, who was wary about the extension of Russian power and sensitive about the dangers of nationalism. Castlereagh and Metternich sought to deter the Tsar from intervention, pointing out that the Turkish Sultan was a legitimate sovereign. When this tactic failed, Castlereagh knew that some measure of intervention was unavoidable, but it was intended as much to restrain Russian aggrandisement as to assist the Greeks. Castlereagh died before such a policy came fully into effect. It was easier for his critics to identify with the Greeks, ignoring something which Castlereagh had never forgotten – that the Greeks of the early nineteenth century were not the Greeks of classical times. A sentimental regard for the Greeks because of an admiration for the culture of ancient Athens was no substitute for a coherent and realistic policy in the Near East. In his policy in the Americas and in his response to the Greek revolt Castlereagh set British policy upon a course which Canning was to exploit with greater histrionic skill but on essentially the same lines. For both men the defence of British interests was the primary purpose of foreign policy. They had differed about the congress system and Britain's commitment to Europe but, by 1822, events had rendered these disagreements far less significant than was once assumed. Canning confessed that when he took over the foreign office after Castlereagh's death he had followed the guidelines laid down in Castlereagh's famous state paper of May 1820.

Liverpool fully supported Castlereagh in his conduct of foreign policy, although, as we have seen, he was capable of asserting his own authority over the impossibility of the Prince Regent's accession to the Holy Alliance. The extent to which backbenchers either understood or supported Castlereagh's policy is another matter. On his return from Vienna, Castlereagh had been enthusiastically applauded in the House of Commons. Members had no doubt that he had served Britain well and that the peace settlement was a good one for Britain. The gains in colonial possessions and the potential for growth in overseas trade were obvious. But Castlereagh never explained the more sophisticated assumptions of his policy to the backbenchers. It was not that he was always indifferent to the impact of public opinion upon policy: at earlier stages of his career he had urged that the reasons for the war with France and the objectives for which Britain was fighting should be unambiguously communicated to the political nation. But it was much more difficult to explain an ongoing relationship with Europe than the direct causes of the war with Napoleon. As it was, the opposition found it convenient to brand his policy as reactionary in inspiration and to talk as if Britain were collaborating with Metternich in imposing rigid and repressive regimes upon the whole of Europe. This misrepresentation reflected ignorance, malice, political opportunism and the fact that Grey and Grenville and their followers were often divided over foreign policy. During the hundred days Grenville and Grey had taken divergent views of what should be done in response to Napoleon's return from Elba. Grenville believed that Napoleon should be rejected and a constitutional monarchy restored in France. However gloomy Grenville had been during the war, he never lost a sober regard for the realities of international relations, which was a consequence of his long experience as foreign secretary. Grey, on the other hand, like other members of the opposition, thought it might be better to acquiesce in a Napoleonic restoration, on the grounds that the French seemed more enthusiastic for Napoleon than for Louis XVIII and that it was unwise for the powers of Europe to expend blood and treasure to restore the Bourbons. Grey feared another long war. Like many old Foxites he could not abandon a respect, possibly a furtive admiration, for Napoleon's military genius. It was also tempting to display a due sensitivity towards the passions of the French people. Grenville, too, loathed the prospect of another long war, but he knew from bitter experience how little Napoleon's professions of peaceful intent were to be relied upon, and he therefore concluded that prompt action seemed best. It was well for the opposition that Waterloo settled the affair quickly. The opposition was divided between realists and idealists. The Holy Alliance and the Greek revolt stimulated further stirrings of the romantic instinct among the opposition. But, while war and foreign policy had imposed strains upon the alliance between Grey and Grenville, the end of the war brought disagreements over domestic policy to the fore, and these were finally to be fatal to the survival of the Grey–Grenville alliance.

Domestic Problems

The transition from a wartime economy to a peacetime one was painful. The end of hostilities was seen as an opportunity for drastic economies in naval and military expenditure; the end of government contracts and the demobilisation of soldiers and sailors caused much distress. Probably about 300 000 men were discharged at the end of the Napoleonic war. It was difficult for the economy to absorb such a number, and in addition the country was experiencing the impact of the early stages of the process of industrialisation. Caution is needed here. Often the pace of industrialisation and the extent to which the country was already urbanised have been exaggerated. Yet although such developments were to reach ever-greater intensity as the century wore on, much of what was happening was without precedent. In the cotton and woollen industries the onset of new technology was creating real problems. In a confused and muddled way framebreaking in the Midlands reflected a widespread distrust of change and a longing for patterns of work which were dying. But the challenges of peace affected agriculture as well as industry. During the war British farmers had enjoyed prosperity. They had responded to the demand for food by exploiting their land to the full. Now, with the coming of peace, they feared what would happen should European grain flood the country. The needs of the farming community loomed large in the consciousness of parliamentarians. In both Lords and Commons the majority had direct links with the landed interest. The political dominance of the landed interest reflected its social and economic supremacy. Only about 1870 did the dominance of industry and commerce become clear and irreversible. In Liverpool's day the majority of politicians, whatever their party, assumed that what was good for the landed interest was good for the country. The prosperity of the farmer seemed the fundamental condition for the prosperity of the nation. No one could contemplate the decline or ruin of the landed community with equanimity. When farmers demanded protection from foreign competition in grain it was inevitable that their cries were heard with sympathy and understanding.

While the farmers feared ruin, financiers, merchants and men of business were worried by the inflation of the war years. The device of paper money had stimulated the economy during the war, but there were prolonged arguments about a return to cash payments. Paper money was denounced as a source of easy wealth; the return to gold was criticised as a recipe for contracting the economy at a time when manufacturers were seeking to expand it. A further controversy raged over the vexed question of the property or income tax. Pitt had always said that it was no more than a temporary expedient for the duration of the war. Now that the war was over it was widely felt that the government should honour Pitt's promise. The income tax was hated as an inquisitorial tax. To many people it seemed obvious that one of the rewards of winning the war should be the end of the detested tax. Although Castlereagh lamented the House of Commons's ignorant impatience of taxation, and although Vansittart, the chancellor of the exchequer, had no wish to rush through abolition, they found the enthusiasm and convictions of the Commons too powerful to withstand. Ignoring pleas for caution, the House insisted that the income tax should go. Its abolition as a result of a backbench rebellion in 1816 only added to the government's difficulties, but the issue was one on which the ministry had no choice but to defer to the judgement of the House of Commons, however defective that judgement may have been.

Liverpool and his colleagues wished, in general, to cut public expenditure, but when they did so they were criticised by Whigs and radicals for not going far enough. A prominent feature of the standard radical critique of the government was that it was wasting large sums of money, particularly on military expenditure. This was a nonsensical charge but it was extensively believed. It was often linked with the claim that Liverpool was planning to establish a military despotism in England. This accusation was spread abroad by the government's opponents when Wellington joined the ministry in 1818. Apart from the ministers, few politicians realised the extent to which the government was hard-pressed for funds. Liverpool had no sympathy for extravagance in public spending, but he knew that there were levels of economy beyond which it was unwise to go. Nevertheless, radical mythology insisted that the government was extracting excessive amounts of money from an oppressed populace. What was true was that indirect taxation pressed more severely upon the poor than upon the rich, but the ministry had been deprived of its only source of direct revenue when the Commons had insisted on ending the income tax. Yet it was common for Liverpool to be denounced for exorbitant waste by radicals who had applauded the abolition of the property tax.

The misrepresentation of the government's intentions was even more blatant over the notorious Corn Law of 1815. Again, much mythology has to be thrust aside. There was nothing novel about a Corn Law. Duties upon imported corn had been levied from time to time since the seventeenth century. In introducing the Corn Law, Liverpool was not preoccupied with devising new methods of raising revenue. He was responding to the vociferous demands of the landed community for protection from foreign competition in corn. Given the dominance of the landed interest within the House of Commons and the prevalent assumption that the wellbeing of the landed community was funda-mental to the well-being of the nation, it was not surprising that the government prohibited the importation of foreign corn until the price of homegrown wheat had reached 80 shillings a quarter. What was relatively new was the radical assertion that such a tax was immoral, in that it was a tax on the food of the poor in order to preserve the status of the rich. Few farmers recognised themselves in the caricatures put out by radical pamphleteers. Many of those who were most committed to the Corn Law were not rich, and the Corn Law of 1815 never gave the farmers the prosperity and security for which they had hoped. The country was now becoming so populous that the dream of self-sufficiency in food was being made more redundant with every year that passed. The farmers found that the Corn Law did not ensure stable markets or stable prices. The small-scale farmer, who could not diversify his activities, discovered that the Corn Law failed to provide that degree of protection which he had sought. Yet to repeal the Corn Law still seemed to be opening the door to ruin. In the 1820s Liverpool introduced a sliding scale in corn, an attempt to adapt the demands of the agricultural lobby to a changing situation. The government could not abandon the farmers to their fate. Although theories of free trade were becoming more prevalent, and the notion of reducing customs and excise duties was becoming more acceptable, it was impossible not to maintain that the protection of agriculture was a special case. As time went by, the expecta-tions hingeing upon the Corn Law altered. In 1815 it had been hoped that a Corn Law would ensure stable markets and stable prices for domestic corn. But many of the defenders of the Corn Law came to see it as little more than a desperate attempt to provide the farmer with a last-ditch security against total disaster. As long as a Corn Law remained on the statute book it would be easier for the farmers to mobilise support and demand government action at times of crisis. To abandon the Corn Law – as distinct from revising it – was commonly interpreted as abdicating responsibility. Radicals agitating against the law were as preoccupied with its place as a symbol of the continued supremacy of the landed interest as they were with the purely economic consequences of the law, most of which they crudely exaggerated and frequently distorted.

Whenever it was faced with evidence of distress, the government's attitude was one of sympathy, coupled with the belief that there was, in fact, little the central government could do to change what seemed to be the given realities of life. During the postwar troubles on Tyneside, Sidmouth showed considerable concern for the welfare of the seamen and keelmen, even when they were involved in strikes. What worried him was the danger that radicals would exploit distress for political ends. The government was not indifferent to the sufferings of the poor, despite their anxiety over the increasing cost of poor relief. The Poor Employment Bill of 1817 demonstrated that Liverpool was willing to take action, within the constraints of the period, to provide work for the poor. But the experiences of the past, and the influence of new theories about the workings of the economy, persuaded the government that it was wholly unrealistic habitually to interfere with the normal patterns of trade and employment. Radical critics were vehement in their demands for less government intervention: it was a fundamental part of the radical creed to affirm that those societies in which governments governed less and taxed little were likely to be the most happy and the most free.

The debate over the condition of the people was made all the more controversial because of the way in which distress and political activity came to be confused. Erratic employment, bad harvests, the impact of new technology, the problems of adjusting to the demands of peace, all created a unique blend of difficulties in the immediate post-Waterloo years. A series of dramatic events made it hard for contemporaries to understand what was going on, and all the easier for alarmists to suggest that the government faced a potentially revolutionary situation. The spectacle of radical demagogues exhorting crowds to demand the reform of parliament or the repeal of the corn laws, at times of widespread hardship, alarmed not only the government but many of the local magistrates up and down the country. Fears of agitation were compounded by memories of the French Revolution, and the tendency to confuse British reformers with French Jacobins. The Spa Fields Riot, the March of the Blanketeers, the Pentridge Rising and, most melodramatically of all, the Peterloo Massacre, have entered the folklore of history, that constantly renewed distortion of the past which seeks to justify some contemporary ideology by misrepresenting the values and the experience of a bygone age. For many years the standard criticism of the Liverpool administration was that it overreacted to a radical threat which had never been as powerful as frightened men had imagined. The radicals were depicted as respectable reformers, whose calls for necessary reform had provoked an outrageous response from a set of nervous reactionaries. The implication was that there was never a real danger of revolution in Britain during the first ten years after the end of the Napoleonic wars. Alarmism and repression were the conventional words to describe and to condemn what had happened.

A quarter of a century ago the debate reopened. It was claimed that there was a genuine revolutionary tradition in Britain which went back to the period of the civil war, that English radicalism was not the creation of the French Revolution, but of a century-and-a-half of history, and that even the revolutionary wing within radicalism was essentially the product of forces which were rooted in the popular perception of the nation's past. Whether this revolutionary tradition was ever on the brink of victory, and the extent to which it could be seen as representing the mainstream of radicalism, were issues which were left studiously vague but emotively powerful. The response of the Liverpool government was still denounced as repressive, though if it were possible to talk of Jeremiah Brandreth, the ill-fated leader of the Pentridge Rising, as a folk hero it was surely understandable that some contemporaries might fear revolution at the time. More recently, debate has shifted to slightly new ground. The majority of English radicals are deemed innocent of complicity in revolutionary plots. The consensus is that revolutionary elements constituted only the extreme fringe of the radical movement, and that they were neither its most representative nor its most effective manifestation. What is now regarded with scepticism is the extent to which the government's response was in any real sense repressive. The Six Acts of 1819, applied in the aftermath of the Cato Street Conspiracy in 1820, have been subjected to a searching examination divorced from the mythology of a hundred and seventy years. They are now seen as little more than gestures, a response to reassure backbench opinion in the House of Commons and conservative opinion in the country, rather than a prelude to a sustained reign of terror. Compared with what Metternich initiated in Austria and Germany they were tame indeed (and even what Metternich instigated fell far short of either the terror or the totalitarianism practised in the twentieth century). The Six Acts were never intended to effect any permanent or substantial change in the pattern of public life. When defending them in the Commons Castlereagh asserted that there was no intention of indefinitely limiting the traditional rights of assembly or petitioning. All the acts did was to strengthen the discretionary powers of the magistrates over local public meetings, to make illegal private drilling and the unauthorised training in the use of arms, and to increase the tax on newspapers, in the hope of limiting the dissemination of radical propaganda. Very few actions were taken under the legislation and one recent authority has dismissed them as an irrelevance.

But even if the acts were important as gestures, rather than a bold initiative affecting the lives of ordinary men and women, they seemed to work. The confidence of the country was restored. Magistrates felt that the government supported them. The propertied members of society believed that something had been done to secure order and to maintain public safety. Much the same thing had happened after Peterloo in August 1819. In private, Liverpool and the ministers were critical of the Manchester magistrates, but they supported them in public. They did so because they knew that without the confidence of the magistracy public order would break down. Its maintenance rested on frail foundations. The resources available to Liverpool for the preservation of law and order were slim. There was no police force, and suggestions that such a force should be set up were usually greeted as evidence that the government was yearning to impose a continental despotism upon freeborn Englishmen. The regular army was the most efficient and impartial force available for controlling riots, but there was considerable reluctance to use it except as a last resort. The yeomanry was often incompetent and politically biased. Had the army and not the yeomanry been used, from the start, to control or to disperse the crowd in Manchester on 16 August 1819, the casualties at Peterloo would have been less, possibly non-existent. The government depended for information and for action upon the magistrates. Ministers knew that the quality and devotion of magistrates varied. There were Tory magistrates and Whig magistrates, even some radical ones. There were magistrates who carried out their duties scrupulously and fairly; there were others who were partial to the point of vehemence. Some were brave, others foolhardy. Some wanted popularity, others a quiet life. The behaviour of the magistrates at Manchester over the Peterloo affair has been frequently criticised. But the sequence of events on that fateful day is far from certain. The magistrates were divided among themselves as to what to do. In retrospect it is easier to blame than to exonerate, but the one thing the magistrates were eager to avoid was a confrontation and a massacre. Panic and incompetence explain what happened, rather than brutal designs upon the common people.

In the past the notion that there was some sort of inevitable correlation between the various highpoints of radical agitation and the climax of the government's response has been overplayed. There was less conspiratorial planning on the part of radicals than fearful magistrates or enthusiastic spies discerned. Similarly, on the government side, there was little coordination. The government was responding, in a rather erratic fashion, to the pattern of events, not dictating it. Nor did Liverpool preside over a policy of systematic repression. He lacked the resources to implement such a policy, even if he had wished to do so. He was so preoccupied with defending the constitution that he was as reluctant to make drastic innovations even for the sake of public tranquillity as he was to depart from the proven path of convention. Innovation was unacceptable. The government saw itself as defending traditional liberties against the wild actions of a minority of disaffected extremists, but there was no desire to depart from precedent and from what a respect for the conventions of the constitution demanded. The ministers' instinct was to play down the critical nature of the domestic situation. Had the advice of the home office been followed by the Manchester magistrates, there would have been no Peterloo incident. Although Sidmouth knew that he had to pay attention to what spies and informers passed on to him – and there was nothing sinister in the employment of such men in the absence of a police force – he was less gullible and less credulous than has sometimes been imagined. He knew that it was easy for informers to exaggerate or for spies to inflate the likelihood of unrest in order to justify and perpetuate their own employment. The danger of revolution was certainly exaggerated, but the government's response fell far short of being alarmist. The danger-signals for a revolution were all absent. The governing elite had not lost confidence in itself or in its right to govern. The nation had not lost confidence in its traditional institutions or in its rulers. The middle and lower orders had not been alienated from the system, though the possibility that they might be antagonised if reform were delayed for too long was a prominent feature of pleas for moderate reform. The economic problems facing the country were not premonitions of disaster but the birth-pangs of a process which was to make possible a better life for the majority of the people. It was also making possible life for more people:

one of the most amazing characteristics of early nineteenth-century Britain was the growth of population. Historians still debate the question of the standard of living, and the causes for the population explosion, but there is no doubt that after 1830 the general trend, maintained to the end of the nineteenth century and into the twentieth, was for living standards to rise.

Not everyone shared in growing prosperity. Progress for some meant disaster for others. The oscillation between boom and slump was erratic, at least until the middle years of the nineteenth century. But while the immediate postwar years saw the propertied orders so anxious about the risk of violent revolution that danger-signals provoked a powerful loyalist reaction, once the crisis was surmounted the commercial and manufacturing classes began to feel that the time had come when their contribution to the evident prosperity of the country, and their loyalty to its institutions when these had seemed under threat, should be rewarded by their being admitted within the pale of the political nation. Rising confidence, not sour envy, was the most potent inspiration behind demands for reform on the part of the new propertied classes. They did not wish to pull down the traditional fabric of government; rather they demanded a share in the political process. Liverpool and his government played a decisive role in bringing this about. They saw off the Jacobinical challenge. Exaggerated though it had been, it had loomed large in the nation's consciousness. But they also did much to win the confidence of the new commercial and manufacturing classes. This was especially true in the 1820s when the policies of Robinson, Huskisson and Peel did much to make businessmen feel that the government was sensitive to the needs of the time, particularly where the stimulation of trade was concerned. It was in this context that Liverpool could be most convincingly seen as a politician who looked back to the world of the eighteenth century and forward to the world of the high nineteenth century. For a government dominated by the landed interest this was no mean feat.

In achieving this, Liverpool played upon memories of the era of Pitt. In one sense this was inevitable, given Liverpool's own background and his experience of politics in the 1790s. But to stand forth as the enemy of Jacobinism and the defender of the country's institutions, while being the invigorator of its commerce, was to act very much in the style of Pitt. Of course, there were those who criticised the government for going too far too quickly, while others urged the ministers to be more bold in their application of new ideas. The ministry's future always looked more vulnerable whenever the Catholic question loomed large or whenever some compromise over the Corn Law seemed in the offing. Liverpool was building on the legacy of Pitt in making the confidence of the crown the bedrock of his political position, and when patiently and tirelessly he sought to win over new men and new groups as friends of the ministry. Although Liverpool lacked the resources of patronage which would have made this task easier, he was careful to ensure that his ministry was perceived as a national administration and not a mere party one. Habit and convenience, rather than accuracy, have permitted his ministry to be called 'Tory'. It was as broadly-based as any in British history. The quest for security went on throughout the fifteen years Liverpool was first minister. He lost no opportunity of winning converts from the opposition, and he was eager to bring forward young men to maintain the vitality of the administration. At times this could cause tension. On one occasion Castlereagh was uneasy about the promotion of Peel. His anxiety was almost certainly caused by the fear that this would strengthen the hands of the anti-Catholic party within the government. The balance between the supporters and opponents of Catholic relief was always a delicate one. Only Liverpool's tact and skill allowed such crises to be happily surmounted.

Liverpool was swift and resourceful in exploiting differences within the ranks of the opposition. The supporters of Grey and Grenville were often divided. The alliance of Grenville and Grey was under constant strain. Both men were eager to keep their party together, partly out of vanity, partly out of loyalty to the memory of the 1806 ministry, partly because they knew that if they went their separate ways the chances of the party getting back into office would be substantially, probably decisively, reduced. The end of the war removed one issue which had always been fraught with problems, but when the postwar years came to be marked by instances of unrest and disorder, Grenville's innate conservatism and his intuitive and gloomy distrust of popular radicalism led him to condone or even to defend actions of the government when the other opposition leaders, despite their own anxieties about radicalism, were venturing to criticise Liverpool's handling of the situation. The old Foxites flattered themselves that they were still the guardians of civil and religious liberty. They liked to project themselves as the only protagonists for traditional Whig virtues. Liverpool was the tool of the crown; the radicals stood for all the lurid excesses of democracy. Feeble though the opposition Whigs were, especially when Ponsonby and Tierney led the party in the Commons, they liked to emerge as the defenders of the liberties of freeborn Englishmen whenever they deemed that these were in danger. But it was often at such times that Grenville would justify or extenuate what the government was doing, arguing that the defence of public order was the first duty of any government faced by the ferocity of the mob or the demands of irresponsible demagogues. By 1817 such differences had effectively ended the alliance between Grenville and his old colleagues. Sadly, Grey and Grenville recognised that they had to part. In 1821 Grenville's benevolent neutrality towards the Liverpool government was transformed into full support. Although Grenville refused to join the administration, chiefly because of his age and failing health, he permitted his supporters to do so. All this is another reminder of the folly of seeing early nineteenth-century politics in terms of two parties contending for office. Fluidity was the order of the day on both sides of the House of Commons.

The opposition seemed further away from office than ever, even though in numbers they had recovered from the depressing experience of the 1790s. The opposition Whigs now numbered about 150 in the House of Commons, when support was at a maximum; about half that number when MPs failed to attend or when the outcome of debate seemed so certain that it appeared pointless to challenge the government. Grey spent much of the time on his Northumbrian estates. He frequently cited his own ill-health or that of his wife for refusing to go up to London to play an active part in parliamentary politics. Even without excuses he lacked heart for the struggle. He detested the government, loathed the radicals, and was sufficiently percipient to realise that there was little chance of the opposition Whigs forcing themselves into office in the foreseeable future. He remained faithful to parliamentary reform in principle, but he was aware that the issue was not a vote-catcher, and he had no wish to see his own support for moderate reform along traditional lines confused with demands for manhood suffrage or annual parliaments. Both Grey and Grenville supported Catholic relief, but after their discomfiture in 1807 they knew that the question was unlikely to bring any immediate benefit to the opposition. One of their disagreements was over the Corn Law. Grey believed that protection for the farmer was necessary and wise and he was uneasy over his eldest son's sympathy for free-trade theories and the possible repeal of the Corn Law. Grenville, on the other hand, had been critical of the Corn Law, seeing it as the means by which the landed interest had used its political influence to raise the cost of living for the poorest sections of the community in a manner which was both immoral and an artificial interference with the market. Some Whigs, such as Brougham, were eager to exploit the Prince Regent's marital problems and his attempts to rid himself of his wife, Caroline of Brunswick, in order to embarrass the ministry, but Grey disliked making much of the issue. He thought the whole episode deplorable, and he knew that to try to make political capital out of it would only heighten the Prince Regent's antagonism towards the opposition Whigs. Grey did not approve of the Prince Regent's conduct, but he shewdly suspected that any short-term gains made by exploiting Caroline's misfortunes would be more than offset by long-term losses.

None of these issues was capable of breaking the confidence which the country gentlemen placed in the Liverpool ministry, or of opening the way for the opposition to return to power. The early 1820s were, in some respects, the nadir of opposition fortunes. The death of Queen Caroline removed one source of embarrassment, much to Liverpool's relief and Grey's satisfaction, but though the tide was beginning to turn in the Commons in favour of Catholic emancipation that question could not be exploited to party advantage, and the known opposition of George IV strengthened the determination of opponents of relief to use their position in the Lords to check any chance of concession. Controversies over the Corn Law, paper money, and poor relief likewise cut across party alignments. Nor was parliamentary reform yet sufficiently relevant to the pressures of day-to-day politics for it to be usefully exploited, even had the Whigs been of one mind on the issue.

A Ministry in Transition

The years 1821 and 1822 saw what amounted to a considerable reshuffle within the Liverpool administration. In January 1822 Sidmouth resigned as home secretary and in August 1822 Castlereagh committed suicide. These events enabled Liverpool to bring forward younger men. Robinson – a relation of Castlereagh and one of his former protégés – became chancellor of the exchequer. Huskisson went to the board of trade. Peel became home secretary. A superficial view might see in these changes a move towards liberalism, and that impression might be heightened by Canning's succession to the place left by Castlereagh, becoming both foreign secretary and leader of the House of Commons. But continuity was the chief feature of British foreign policy, although Canning was more adept than his predecessor in communicating his enthusiasms to the public. Any difference was one of character and temperament, rather than of policy. Canning was not, in fact, more liberal than Castlereagh. Like Castlereagh he supported Catholic relief, and, like Castlereagh, he did so on terms which favoured the so-called veto, by which Catholic emancipation was to be accompanied by securities for the establishment in church and state by giving the British crown the right to scrutinise the appointment of Catholic clergy. Such compromise schemes came to nothing. Although English Catholics were prepared to acquiesce in them they were rejected by most Irish Catholics, who resented the possibility that the royal veto might transform the Catholic church in Ireland into a bastion of unionism. Canning was also opposed to any sweeping measure of parliamentary reform. 1822 cannot be seen as a turning-point. As long as Liverpool remained at the head of the ministry he determined the general thrust of policy. The improving economic performance of the country and the demise of the Jacobinical threat gave Liverpool greater freedom in following those policies which were more suitable to times of prosperity than to times of stress. There was no transformation in ideology or practice. Canning served Liverpool well, but the distrust of Canning which was deeply ingrained in some sections of the administration erupted after Liverpool's death. When Canning formed a ministry, he did so at the price of dropping some Tories – both Peel and Wellington refused to serve under Canning – and turning to the more conservative Whigs. The fluidity of political alignments was further confirmed, and had Canning lived, the evolution of party might have followed a very different course.

While Canning may be deemed a conservative with a flair for public relations and a keen eye for changes in both public opinion and the political climate, it is much harder to place Peel on an appropriate point in the conventional conservative/liberal spectrum. In some ways Peel was liberal. He was associated with monetary reform. He carried through an impressive series of legal and penal reforms. In questions pertaining to commerce and the economy he was responsive to liberal thinking and eager to take the country further down the road to free trade: a course which could still be seen as following in the steps of Pitt rather than anticipating the doctrines of Richard Cobden. But on the Catholic question Peel was conservative. He was a sincere Anglican who prized the traditional relationship between church and state. He rejected anything which would weaken the establishment. He believed that full membership of the political nation ought to be synonymous with membership of the Anglican communion. He distrusted the power of the pope and the influence of the Jesuits. He never advocated religious intolerance or persecution: he did not object to Catholics having the freedom to practise their religion, but he was suspicious of the political consequences of admitting them to the political nation. Two of the most forthright and cogent opponents of Catholic emancipation were Eldon and Peel. Both argued that the case against the admission of Catholics to full political rights rested on the benefits which the country had gained from the 1688 Revolution. To admit Catholics to parliament would be the first breach in the Revolution Settlement; once it was achieved others would follow. For similar reasons Peel, like Eldon, opposed any sweeping measure of parliamentary reform. Liverpool was not the only member of his government to be poised between the world of the eighteenth century and the world of the Victorian era.

Talk of liberal Toryism must be carefully restricted to certain areas of policy. The 1820s saw the reduction of many customs duties, the simplification of many of those which remained, the end of the navigation laws, and the repeal of the anti-combination laws, though the repeal of the latter was followed by a law imposing restraints upon the formation of trade unions. Yet however much Robinson and Huskisson felt that they were releasing the resources of the nation in order to achieve commercial success and economic advancement, they acted as politicians and not as theorists. It is questionable whether the ministers fully grasped all the implications of the new economic thinking. In some ways the new theories confirmed the rightness of what ministers were inclined to do by the exercise of old-fashioned political intuition. There was a cautious and pragmatic quality about the reforms inaugurated by Liverpool and his colleagues. They had no ambitious and comprehensive scheme of reform. Though they were eager to show that they were sensitive to the needs of the new commercial and mercantile interests, political survival meant that they could never forget the duty they owed to the landed interest or the overriding need for any government to keep the country gentlemen happy. Disillusionment with the Corn Law of 1815 prodded Liverpool into introducing the sliding scale, which had, in any event, been what the ministry had tended to favour in 1815, had they been able to persuade the landed interest of the advantages of such a provision, rather than a fixed level below which the prohibition of imported grain was absolute. The sliding scale was an attempt to please those who looked to the government for protection and to accommodate those who were claiming that the Corn Law distorted the normal patterns of trade. The ministers saw nothing inconsistent in moving towards freer trade while trying to honour their obligations to the farming interest. They were preoccupied with meeting the needs of conflicting interests, and with resolving conflicts of interest with a regard for the wellbeing of the nation as a whole. This was much more important than seeking to put into effect any set of theories in a manner smacking of dogmatism.

Liberal Toryism was not, therefore, some self-evident creed to which the government arbitrarily turned in 1822; just as the ministry may be regarded as Tory only in a carefully limited sense, so their liberalism was valid only within a circumscribed range of meaning. Continuity was the clue to the ministry's behaviour. As confidence grew and domestic dangers diminished, Liverpool felt it was realistic to give greater scope to presumptions which had been there from the beginning. The example of Pitt loomed larger than the theories of Smith, Ricardo and Malthus, though such theories could be cited to give more articulate justification to policies which were thought practicable, profitable and safe. Just as the Catholic question cut across conventional alignments, so there were vigorous debates among the economic theorists on matters such as paper money, the resumption of cash payments, the Corn Law and the general subject of free trade. Neither government nor opposition should be seen exclusively or primarily in free-trade terms. There was a growing assumption that the less governments interfered with trade the better, but Liverpool did not preside over a wholesale or systematic conversion to doctrinaire free-trade principles. He merely sought to implement policies which enabled the government to claim that it was helping trade to find its own level, the energies of the people being the chief agency in any recognisable improvement. Liverpool was unable to find any answer to the problems of poor relief. There was general agreement, transcending the partisan alignments of the House of Commons, that the cost of poor relief was prohibitive, but only when Grey's ministry responded to the rural disorders of 1830 was the scene set for the amendment of the Poor Law in 1834.

Similarly, nothing changed Liverpool's conviction that the British constitution was such a blessing that it had to be preserved inviolate for future generations. The constitution was thought to be fundamental to the achievement of social advancement, improved trade and sustained prosperity. Although the debate over the disfranchisement of Grampound showed that the government could contemplate cautious redistribution in a very limited fashion there was never any likelihood that Liverpool would seize the initiative on the subject of parliamentary reform. Later, amid the bitterness of the struggle over the Great Reform Act, Tories regretted that Liverpool had not carried a modest measure of reform in the 1820s. Men of a conservative frame of mind came to believe that moderate parliamentary reform under Liverpool might have saved the country from the horrors of the crises over Catholic emancipation and the reform of parliament. But such feelings were expressions of regret for the present and of fears for the future: they did not reflect what had been politically possible before 1827. Liverpool had not taken up parliamentary reform because he could not discern either a sufficiently powerful demand for it or a commensurate political benefit to be gained from it. To the end of his ministry the issue which posed the greatest threat to the stability of the government and to the continued pattern of politics was the question with which ministers had lived throughout the lifetime of the administration: Catholic emancipation. The Catholic question posed the greatest challenge to the broadly-based party which Liverpool had built up with such painstaking care. After both Liverpool and Canning were dead, O'Connell seized the initiative with such skill and daring that Catholic relief first demoralised and then fragmented the party which had dominated politics for so long.

While Liverpool's achievement must be seen in essentially traditionalist terms, his long premiership saw several changes which showed that while he had restored the Pittite tradition he had moved out of the shadow of the Younger Pitt. Liverpool was in a much stronger position than Pitt had been in dealing with the King. This was not only because the influence of the crown had declined but because, unlike Pitt, Liverpool could rely upon his colleagues following him out of office were he forced to resign, either because of defeat in the Commons or because of the withdrawal of royal confidence. It was the latter possibility which posed the more dangerous threat to the continuation of the ministry. Liverpool could accept defeats in the House of Commons on certain issues without losing the general approval of MPs, but George IV always remained a touchy and treacherous master. Liverpool's hand in dealing with the King was strengthened by the knowledge that if George IV forced him to resign this would mean a complete change of ministers, not just a reshuffle under a new head. Collective appointment and collective resignation were now features of the political system: they had not been so at the close of the eighteenth century. Liverpool presided over a remarkably harmonious ministry. Without any desire for doctrinaire innovation, he had established that primacy for the first lord of the treasury which Pitt had eventually recognised as desirable but which he had been unable to achieve. Liverpool's insistence on collective responsibility grew from his concern for the effectiveness of government. Innovations were made for reasons of practicability, not dogma. The 1820s also saw the acceptance of formed opposition as a valid and permanent element in political activity. This had been a long and complex process. Despite the frustrations of the opposition Whigs, the idea of 'His Majesty's Opposition' came of age in the 1820s. It did much to simplify the notion of politics. But it was not yet synonymous with a fully developed and completely mature version of a two-party system. It represented an acceptance of party, but party remained a loose and vulnerable organism. General elections were still appeals by the king and his ministers for a vote of confidence from the political nation, not the means by which the electorate chose between competing alternatives for office. The majority of seats remained uncontested. Agreed returns were common. The most dramatic victories were often won, not by an opposition seeking to gain office, but by ministers seeking to confirm their hold on power. The confidence of the king was the most influential single element in winning the confidence of the political nation. Grey was to win two dramatic victories as prime minister because he was able to appeal to the political nation for a renewal of support over a highly controversial matter with the confidence of the King to back him up. Yet in 1835 William IV could not do for Peel what his father had done for Pitt in 1784. The crown could no longer exercise the sort of electoral influence which had been so significant in the eighteenth century. Although the party system only came of age after the 1867 Reform Act and although politics only began to manifest certain characteristics in the 1880s, the Liverpool years were at once the apotheosis of traditionalism and a seedbed for the emergence of developments which over a period of half a century eventually led to the party system of the late Victorian era.

The broadly-based notion of party, which traditional thinking condoned and which Liverpool had practised with such success, was nevertheless vulnerable to change. Much depended on the king and prime minister working in harmony, each possessing the confidence of the other. Liverpool endured much from George IV but he knew that the King had no real alternative minister. George IV could not risk a change of first minister without precipitating a far-reaching shake-up in government, which was the last thing he wanted. The dissolution of the Tory party after Liverpool's stroke in 1827 highlights the decisive nature of his own contribution. Had Canning lived, he might have established a broadly-based ministry on a rather different base – a coalition of liberal Tories and conservative Whigs. But Canning's death and the collapse of Goderich's ministry prevented this new alignment from having the chance to prove itself in office, and it was in office that significant transformations of party were most likely to occur. Wellington sought to revive a ministry which was conservative in its stance, both at home and abroad, but his ministry never recovered from the crisis provoked by O'Connell's agitation for Catholic relief and which was only partly resolved by the passage of Catholic emancipation. The Tories were left embittered and divided; Wellington and Peel were denounced as apostates. It was this which compelled Wellington to make his ill-starred bid for the renewed confidence of the Ultra-Tories, and the failure of that strategem led to the fall of Wellington's ministry and Grey's assumption of office in 1830.

Grey's ministry was not a straightforward Whig administration. It contained former Canningites, Huskissonites and independents, Tories such as Ripon, who later returned to the conservative fold under Peel, and Whigs who looked fondly back to the age of Fox. It was moulded by the need to pass a reform bill more than by any other consideration. All this was a stark reminder that while party and opposition, collective responsibility, collective appointment and collective resignation, had all become conventions of political life, neither the 'Whig' nor the 'Tory' parties were monolithic, wholly coherent, well-disciplined or permanent. Only when the popular and extraparliamentary aspects of politics became more important, with the expansion of the electorate, did political parties develop the organisation which enabled them to discipline their followers and to claim for themselves a continuity which disguised the manner in which the beliefs, policies, character and conduct of parties have changed. Names preserve a semblance of legitimate descent and organisation suggests continuity, but parties are the children of miscegenation, not of pure descent, and they have always been exposed to the vagaries of fortune and the divisive impact of controversies, whether these have been over Catholic emancipation, the repeal of the corn laws, Irish home rule, tariff reform, or the need to form coalition governments at times of crisis. Realignment is often talked about today, but it is harder to accomplish than in the days when the behaviour of a motley pattern of parliamentary groups decided the fate of ministries and changed the mode and style of party.

Liverpool's achievement showed that traditionalism in politics could still accomplish much. Just as Pitt had demonstrated the vitality of traditional assumptions, so Liverpool had revived and renewed them by his mastery of men and events. But the fate of the Tory party after his death reveals the limits which must be placed upon his achievement and the necessity to judge him by the standards of his own time. What appears to a later age as an era of confusion was merely the repetition of a familiar pattern. Instead of looking for false continuity or for dubious anticipations of later developments historians should evaluate the past on its own terms. Judged by the standards of their age both Pitt and Liverpool were consummate politicians. They showed that the traditional system could survive the challenge of war, the threat of revolution, the impact of unprecedented social change. Yet each appeal to the familiar chain of belief and practice was marked by an openness to new developments which enabled transition to take place while continuity was preserved. When the final crisis of the old order came, with the struggle over the great Reform Bill, it was surmounted without any breach in historical continuity and in a fashion which, when compared with the French Revolution, was marked by courtesy and restraint. However vehemently they debated the issues or assailed each other with all the acerbity of rivals for place and power, the leading politicians of the time regarded their primary loyalty as being that which they owed to the constitution. Preserving the system was dear to both Tory and Whig. They were agreed on essentials. They disagreed over what was the best means of preserving the country's institutions and familiar liberties, not the desirability of such an objective. When conventions changed they did so within the context of loyalty to a received tradition of political behaviour. Renovation, not innovation, was the most effective rallying cry for reformers.

In renewing the familiar pattern of politics, and in allowing the majority of politically alert Englishmen to feel that the constitution merited the respect and affection of the nation, Pitt and Liverpool enabled change to be accomplished in a fashion which preserved all that was best in the old while cautiously opening the door to the new. They laid the foundations for Grey's achievement in 1832. They believed that the essential prerequisite for constructive politics was a regard for the parliamentary system and that distinctive style of monarchy which had evolved since 1689. The terms on which the great debate over parliamentary reform was conducted were the greatest of tributes to the vitality, not the exhaustion, of the traditional system. It was sufficiently soundly based to be able to contain a measure of adaptation. Restoration and renewal were the hallmarks of reform in 1832. Grey and his colleagues showed a traditional concern for the security of property as the surest foundation for liberty. The triumph of reform owed much to the crown and to the aristocracy. Representative government proved the best safeguard against premature democracy and the surest preparation of the way to ultimate democracy. To contemporaries its greatest virtue was that it enabled the king's government to be carried on. It was the performance of that function which was the decisive criterion by which the efficacy of the system was judged. Throughout the era of Pitt and Liverpool the three essentials of good government were seen as residing in the protection of personal liberty, the security of private property, and a modest level of taxation. Such aims were less visionary than the rights of man, but they were a surer guide amid the turmoils of war and change, and they constitute the best clues to an understanding of the men who won the war and enabled the nation to withstand the trials of peace.

FURTHER READING

Although historians no longer write under the shadow of Namier it remains true that a familiarity with his work is fundamental to an understanding of the eighteenth century, even if his conclusions have to be judiciously qualified. *The Structure of Politics at the Accession of George III* (London, 2nd edn, 1957) and *England in the Age of the American Revolution* (London, 2nd edn, 1961) should be consulted, as should be the essays on monarchy and the party system and the country gentlemen in parliament printed in *Crossroads of Power* (London, 1962). Revisionist views of the early eighteenth-century Tory party may be found in L. Colley, *In Defiance of Oligarchy* (Cambridge, 1982), and E. Cruickshanks, *Political Untouchables* (London, 1979), but there is some penetrating comment in P. D. G. Thomas, 'Party Politics in Eighteenth-century Britain: Some Myths and a Touch of Reality', *British Journal for Eighteenth-century Studies* X (1987). J. C. D. Clark, *The Dynamics of Change* (Cambridge, 1982), demonstrates that the 1750s were a watershed in party development, and the same author has emphasised the significance of discontinuity in 'A General Theory of Party, Opposition, and Government 1688–1832', *Historical Journal* XXIII (1980). The influence of religious issues and traditionalist thinking is shown in J. C. D. Clark, *English Society 1688–1832* (Cambridge, 1985). R. Pares, *King George III and the Politicians* (Oxford, 1953), and H. Butterfield, *George III and the Historians* (London, 1957), are still enlightening. B. W. Hill, *British Parliamentary Parties 1742–1832* (London, 1985), is preoccupied with continuity, while F. O'Gorman, *The Rise of Party in England: the Rockingham Whigs* (London, 1975), and the same author's *The Emergence of the British Two-party System* (London, 1982), also belong to the school preoccupied with evolution. J. J. Sack, *From Jacobite to Conservative: Reaction and Orthodoxy in Britain* (Cambridge, 1993), is provocative and illuminating. F. O'Gorman, *Voters, Patrons and Parties* (Oxford 1989), is a comprehensive account of the unreformed system which demonstrates its vitality as well as its idiosyncrasies.

J. Brewer, *Party Ideology and Popular Politics at the Accession of George III* (Cambridge, 1976) attempts to interweave high politics and popular movements but, though he throws out several novel ideas about Wilkes, two key studies of Wilkes remain: G. Rude, *Wilkes and Liberty* (Oxford, 1962), and I. R. Christie, *Wilkes, Wyvill and Reform* (London, 1962). The best biography of Wilkes is P. D. G. Thomas, *John Wilkes, a Friend to Liberty* (Oxford, 1996). There are two good biographies of George III: S. Ayling, *George III*

(London, 1972), and J. Brooke, *King George III* (London, 1972). The legend of Bute is dissected by J. Brewer, 'The Misfortunes of Lord Bute', *Historical Journal* XVI (1973). For approaches to ideology see H. T. Dickinson, *Liberty and Property* (London, 1977), J. Brewer, 'Rockingham, Burke and Whig Political Argument', *Historical Journal* XVIII (1975), and F. O'Gorman, *Edmund Burke: His Political Philosophy* (London, 1973). Two biographies of Burke are particularly useful: S. Ayling, *Edmund Burke: His Life and Opinions* (London, 1988), and C. C. O'Brien, *The Great Melody* (London, 1992). The American crisis is dealt with by I. R. Christie, *Crisis of Empire* (London, 2nd edn, 1974), J. W. Derry, *English Politics and the American Revolution* (London, 1976), B. Donoughue, *British Politics and the American Revolution: the Path to War* (London, 1964), and H. T. Dickinson (ed.), *Britain and the American Revolution* (London, 1998). P. D. G. Thomas's trilogy is a masterly study of British policy towards the American colonies: *British Politics and the Stamp Act Crisis* (Oxford, 1975), *The Townshend Duties Crisis* (Oxford, 1987) and *Tea Party to Independence* (Oxford, 1991). P. D. G. Thomas, *Lord North* (London, 1976), and I. R. Christie, *The End of North's Ministry* (London, 1958), are essential reading. For the crisis of 1782–3, J. A. Cannon, *The Fox–North Coalition* (Cambridge, 1969), is indispensable, as is M. D. George, 'Fox's Martyrs: the General Election of 1784' printed in I. R. Christie (ed.), *Essays in Modern History* (London, 1968). I. R. Christie, *Myth and Reality in Late Eighteenth-century British Politics* (London, 1970), is an excellent collection of papers.

   For the politics of the 1780s, P. Kelly, 'British Parliamentary Politics 1784–86', *Historical Journal* XVII (1974), D. G. Barnes, *George III and William Pitt* (Stanford, 1939), J. Holland Rose, *William Pitt and National Revival* (London, 1911), are all useful, but J. Ehrman, *The Younger Pitt: the Years of Acclaim* (London, 1969) is an authoritative account. L. G. Mitchell, *Charles James Fox and the Disintegration of the Whig Party* (Oxford, 1971), J. W. Derry, *The Regency Crisis and the Whigs* (Cambridge, 1963), D. Ginter, *Whig Organization in the General Election of 1790* (Berkeley, 1967), and F. O'Gorman, *The Whig Party and the French Revolution* (London, 1967), chart the fortunes of the opposition from a variety of viewpoints. J. W. Derry, *Charles James Fox* (London, 1972), and L. G. Mitchell, *Charles James Fox* (Oxford, 1992), survey the whole of Fox's career with a blend of criticism and sympathy. For the impact of the French Revolution, P. A. Brown, *The French Revolution in English History* (London, 1918), remains valuable, but there is a multidimensional perspective on this subject in H. T. Dickinson (ed.), *Britain and the French Revolution* (London, 1989). Popular radicalism is dealt with by E. P. Thompson, *The Making of the English Working Class* (London, 1964), A. Goodwin, *The Friends of Liberty* (London, 1979), and M. I. Thomis and P. Holt, *Threats of Revolution in Britain* (London, 1977). D. E. Brewster and N. McCord, 'Some Labour Troubles in the 1790s in North East England', *Review of Social History* XIII (1968), show how local studies can cast light on larger issues. For parliamentary reform G. Veitch, *The Genesis of Parliamentary Reform* (London, 1913), may still be recommended, but J. A. Cannon, *Parliamentary Reform* (Cambridge, 1973), is indispensable because of the breadth and incisiveness of its approach.

J. Ehrman, *The Younger Pitt: the Reluctant Transition* (London, 1983), and *The Younger Pitt: the Consuming Struggle* (London, 1996) deals magisterially with Pitt's response to the Revolutionary and Napoleonic Wars, but J. Holland Rose, *William Pitt and the Great War* (London, 1911), still provides much information and sane comment. J. Mori, *William Pitt and the French Revolution* (Keele, 1997), highlights the complexities of Pitt's attitudes to the challenge of the Revolution, while E. V. Macleod, *A War of Ideas* (Aldershot, 1998), discusses the interplay between ideology and diplomacy. The loyalist movement may be studied in E. C. Black, *The Association: the British Extra-parliamentary Organization* (Cambridge, Mass., 1963), R. R. Dozier, *For King, Constitution and Country: the English Loyalists and the French Revolution* (London, 1983), D. Ginter, 'The Loyalist Association Movement of 1792–93', *Historical Journal* IX (1966), A. Mitchell, 'The Association Movement of 1792–93', *Historical Journal* IV (1961), and J. R. Western, 'The Volunteer Movement as an anti-Revolutionary Force', *English Historical Review* XXXI (1956). There is some illuminating comment on the growth of popular political awareness in L. Colley, *Britons* (Yale, 1992). Three articles by C. Emsley are especially useful: 'The London Insurrection of December 1792', *Journal of British Studies* XVII (1978); 'The Home Office and Its Sources of Information and Investigation', *English Historical Review* XCIV (1979); and 'An Aspect of Pitt's "Terror": Prosecutions for Sedition During the 1790s', *Social History* VI (1981). The same author's *British Society and the French Wars* (London, 1979), is a good general account. P. Mackesy, *The Strategy of Overthrow* (London, 1974), and *War Without Victory* (Oxford, 1984), contain excellent analyses of the strategic problems of the war together with perceptive coverage of their political ramifications. For the Irish Union G. C. Bolton, *The Passing of the Irish Act of Union* (Oxford, 1966), long dominated the scene, but P. M. Geoghegan, *The Irish Act of Union* (Dublin, 1999), is shrewd and sensitive, combining a sharp eye for detail with a command of the larger issues.

A. D. Harvey, *Britain in the Early Nineteenth Century* (London, 1978), together with his article 'The Ministry of All the Talents', *Historical Journal* XV (1972), demolishes much sentimental legend about the period. P. Ziegler, *Addington* (London, 1965), P. Jupp, *Lord Grenville* (Oxford, 1985), D. Gray, *Spencer Perceval* (Manchester, 1963), and R. A. Melikan, *John Scott, Lord Eldon* (Cambridge, 1999), do much by way of rehabilitation. J. J. Sack, *The Grenvillites* (Chicago, 1979), M. Roberts, *The Whig Party 1807–12* (London, 1939), and A. Mitchell, *The Whigs in Opposition* (Oxford, 1967), cover the misfortunes of the opposition. For the later stages of the French wars, R. Glover, *Britain at Bay* (London, 1973), R. Glover, *Peninsular Preparation* (Cambridge, 1963), D. Gates, *The Spanish Ulcer* (London, 1986), R. Parkinson, *The Peninsular War* (London, 1973), and R. Muir, *Britain and the Defeat of Napoleon* (Yale, 1996), treat the military issues.

The politics of the Liverpool era are analysed in W. R. Brock, *Lord Liverpool and Liberal Toryism* (Cambridge, 1941), a pioneering study, and in J. Cookson, *Lord Liverpool's Administration* (Edinburgh, 1975) and B. Hilton, *Corn, Cash, Commerce* (Oxford, 1977). N. Gash has written admirably about Liverpool, both in *Aristocracy and People* (London, 1979), and *Lord Liverpool* (London, 1984). The best treatment of the Catholic issue is G. I. T. Machin,

The Catholic Question in English Politics (Oxford, 1964). P. Jupp, British Politics on the Eve of Reform (Basingstoke, 1998), analyses the context to Wellington's administration comprehensively and thoughtfully. B. Fontana, Rethinking the Politics of Commercial Society (Cambridge, 1985) deals with the debate between the theorists of the time. R. J. White, Waterloo to Peterloo (London, 1957), F. O. Darvall, Popular Disturbances and Public Order in Regency England (London, 1934), D. Read, Peterloo: the Massacre and Its Background (Manchester, 1957), and R. Walmsley, Peterloo: the Case Reopened (Manchester, 1969), provide ample and varied material on the interrelation between political and social questions. The essays of N. McCord, J. A. Cannon and J. W. Derry in J. A. Cannon (ed.), The Whig Ascendancy (London, 1981), should also be consulted. N. McCord, 'The Seamen's Strike of 1815 in North-east England', Economic History Review, 2nd series, XXI (1968), is excellent on the government's attitude to popular disturbances.

Foreign policy in the late eighteenth century is authoritatively handled by J. Black, British Foreign Policy in an Age of Revolutions (Cambridge, 1994), while for the later part of the period covered in this book two classic accounts remain invaluable: C. Webster, The Foreign Policy of Castlereagh (2 vols, London, 2nd edn, 1963), and H. W. V. Temperley, The Foreign Policy of Canning (London, 2nd edn, 1966). A number of biographies may also be commended: C. J. Bartlett, Castlereagh (London, 1966), J. W. Derry, Castlereagh (London, 1976), W. Hinde, Canning (London, 1973), P. J. V. Rolo, George Canning (London, 1965), N. Gash, Mr Secretary Peel (London, 1961), W. R. Jones, Prosperity Robinson (London, 1967), E. Longford, Wellington, Pillar of State (London, 1972), E. A. Smith, Lord Grey (Oxford, 1990), J. W. Derry, Charles, Earl Grey (Oxford, 1992), E. A. Smith, George IV (Yale, 1999).

INDEX

161